Discovery of a Lost Bronze Age

BAN CHIANG

An exhibition
organized by
The University Museum,
University of Pennsylvania

The Smithsonian Institution
Traveling Exhibition Service

The National Museums Division,
Department of Fine Arts,
Thailand

by
Joyce C. White
with contributions from
Pisit Charoenwongsa
Ward H. Goodenough

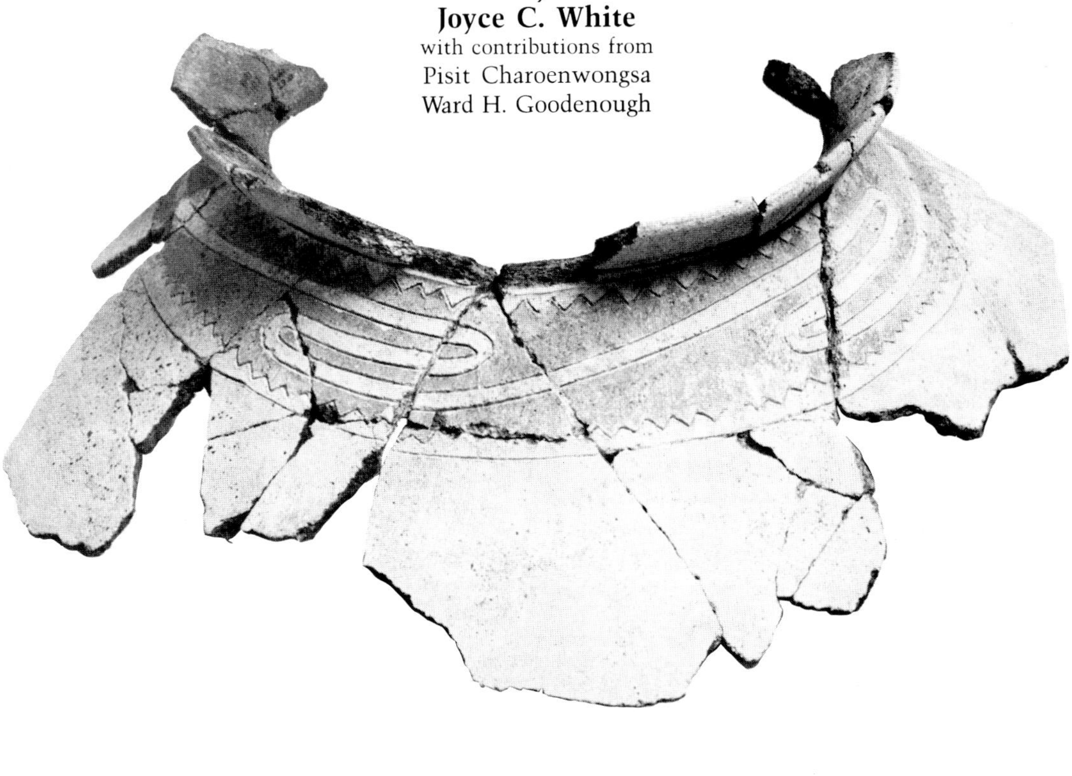

Published by The University Museum, University of Pennsylvania, and the Smithsonian Institution Traveling Exhibition Service (SITES). SITES is a program activity of the Smithsonian Institution that organizes and circulates exhibitions on art, history, and science to institutions in the United States and abroad.

Library of Congress Cataloging in Publication Data

White, Joyce C., 1952–
Ban Chiang: discovery of a lost Bronze Age.

Includes bibliographical references.
1. Bronze age—Thailand—Ban Chiang—Exhibitions.
2. Ban Chiang (Thailand)—Antiquities—Exhibitions.
3. Thailand—Antiquities—Exhibitions. I. Pisit Charoenwongsa. II. Goodenough, Ward Hunt.
III. University of Pennsylvania. University Museum.
IV. Smithsonian Institution. Traveling Exhibition Service. V. Thailand. Kǫng Phiphitthaphan Sathān hæng Chat. VI. Title.
GN778.32.T5W54 1982 959.3'02'07409593 82-19318
ISBN 0-8122-7971-2
ISBN 0-8122-1137-5 (pbk.)

Cover: Excavation at Ban Chiang with superimposed images of cat. nos. 34, 31, 25, and 92.

Inside covers: Front, cat. no. 149 (detail); back, cat. no. 153 (detail).

Distributed by the University of Pennsylvania Press
3933 Walnut Street
Philadelphia, PA 19104

CONTENTS

Exhibition Sponsors

We are grateful to the following organizations without whose generous financial assistance this exhibition and catalogue would not have been possible.

Pew Memorial Trust

Union Oil Company of California Foundation

Thai Farmers Bank

Sukum Navapan Foundation

Siam Commercial Bank

The Ford Foundation

Asian Cultural Council

Pan American World Airways

We are honored to acknowledge Her Royal Highness, Princess Maha Chakri Sirindhorn of Thailand, as the honorary patron of this exhibition.

FORWORD

The University Museum's excavation at Ban Chiang was undoubtedly our most significant field research in the past decade. Dr. Chester Gorman was a valued colleague at the Museum whose untimely death meant much to all of us both personally and professionally, and it is with a mixed sense of sadness and pride that I welcome you to the Ban Chiang exhibition. There is sadness in that Chet cannot see what his students and colleagues have done to bring this spectacular site to the attention of the world. Our pride comes as a product of having been able to bring the exhibition to fruition.

Inevitably, the scientific method and a continuation of research mean that perceptions once prevalent about Ban Chiang will change. They have certainly done this during the creation of the exhibition, and we expect more as the work is finalized in Philadelphia and Bangkok. This is the price we pay for actively inquiring into the early history of mankind. Thus, what you will see in the exhibition is one window into the past—the one through which we look today. Surely the future will bring other changes—some minor, many major—in our understanding of Ban Chiang and the history of Southeast Asia. What is not going to change, however, are the fundamentals of scientific inquiry and this process is, we hope, one of the predominant themes we have developed in the course of telling you this fascinating story of unexpected discovery and the search for greater understanding.

The Ban Chiang Project developed as something of a model of both interdisciplinary and international cooperation. We owe special thanks to Khun Dejo Savanananda, the Director General of the Fine Arts Department, for his unfailing support and understanding of the difficulties we have faced in the absence of Dr. Gorman. His colleague Khun Chira Chongkol, the Head of the National Museums Division, very capably and admirably arranged for the loan of objects from Thailand that has so measurably enriched the exhibition. It is also worth noting that the Government of Thailand has allowed virtually the entire Ban Chiang collection to remain at The University Museum until we are satisfied that sufficient analysis has been completed for a final report to be prepared. The excavated material will then be returned to Thailand as will the bilingual exhibition which will be exhibited in its country of origin at the close of the U.S. tour.

Robert Dyson
Director
The University Museum,
University of Pennsylvania

When Dr. Chester Gorman first came to the Smithsonian Institution Traveling Exhibition Service in the spring of 1979 to discuss a possible exhibition based on the archaeological work at a remote site in northeastern Thailand, Ban Chiang was only an exotic-sounding name, somewhat difficult to pronounce. However, SITES felt the project had enormous possibilities and sensed its importance through the contagious excitement which Dr. Gorman generated whenever he spoke about this new discovery. Soon after, SITES embarked on a cooperative venture with The University Museum and the Fine Arts Department of the Government of Thailand. This joint effort has now had its professional rewards in the manifestation of an important new exhibition, as well as the first catalogue on the Ban Chiang site. Additionally, the exhibition has served as a catalyst for stepped-up analysis of the enormous amount of scientific data which resulted from this model multidisciplinary excavation.

The careful digging of this site during the official field seasons of 1974–1975 by teams of scientists from throughout the world, and the subsequent analysis of data in the laboratory, represent the kind of scientific investigation and international cooperation the Smithsonian encourages, and is eager to be partner to. I am pleased that SITES will be able to share the results of this important project with museum visitors throughout the United States. The exhibition and its catalogue also represent the first general introduction of Ban Chiang to the public at large. We hope that the catalogue will serve as an important reference for both the public and the academic community recording the extraordinary finds at this site. For the scholar, it represents the first pictorial record of the most important objects from the excavation, as well as an account of the basic chronology. For the general reader, it is an archaeological detective story of the best kind.

What the audience will not readily glean from viewing this exhibition and experiencing its presentation is the coordination, care, complicated arrangements, and international negotiations attendant to such a project. SITES Coordinator Martha Cappelletti has handled, with great talent and intelligence, the many and varied parts of this SITES undertaking, and is responsible for making this project a reality. Every director should be so blessed as to have such creative and thorough assistance.

Until now, the public has only received tantalizing glimpses of this important prehistoric culture. The first explosive story appeared in *National Geographic* in 1971 and generated enormous enthusiasm. The information, however, was less than complete because basic research on the Ban Chiang site had yet to be finished. While this exhibition and catalogue will fill many of the gaps, the "case" is never closed on archaeological detective stories, and the clues continue to be revealed. This is only the beginning.

Peggy Loar
Director
Smithsonian Institution
Traveling Exhibition Service

ACKNOWLEDGEMENTS

Ban Chiang: Discovery of a Lost Bronze Age is an undertaking which would not have been possible without the dedicated work of many staff members and volunteers in a number of organizations on both sides of the Pacific Ocean, all of whom cannot possibly be thanked here. I hope they know their behind-the-scenes efforts are deeply appreciated.

First and foremost, this catalogue is dedicated to the late Dr. Chester Gorman whose pioneering work in the field of Southeast Asian archaeology will remain a most significant contribution for years to come. There are no words to convey the loss his friends and colleagues feel at his death, nor the great loss it means to the science of archaeology. This exhibition was Dr. Gorman's dream, and we are proud to have played a part in its realization.

I would like to thank the Department of Fine Arts of the Government of Thailand whose interest in the prehistory of the country enabled the excavation to take place, and its Director-General, Dejo Savanananda, whose continued cooperation has facilitated the development of this exhibition. His personal hospitality made the complicated but necessary negotiations more enjoyable. Chira Chongkol, the Director of the National Museums Division, generously opened her museum's collections to us to supplement the excavated objects from Ban Chiang and arranged for the shipment of the loans to the United States. While we were in Thailand, and later at The University Museum in Philadelphia, the project benefitted enormously from the expertise of Pisit Charoenwongsa of the Department of Fine Arts' Archaeology Division who was co-director of the excavation with Dr. Gorman. His introduction appears in this catalogue. I wish to thank all of the staff members of the Thai Department of Fine Arts and the National Museum who made our visit so successful. I would especially like to thank Dr. Sippanondha Ketudat, former Minister of Education, whose personal assistance aided in the funding of the exhibition.

When Dr. Gorman became ill and was unable to accompany me to Thailand for the initial loan negotiations, it was recommended that I contact Joyce White, a student of Dr. Gorman's who had been working for two years at Ban Chiang. This turned out to be one of the most fortuitous introductions possible, because Joyce has since become the curatorial guiding light of the exhibition, without whom we would have had to abandon the project. Her assistance in Bangkok, through the generosity of Betty Starr Cummin, was greatly appreciated. Upon Chet's untimely death, Joyce returned to the United States and immersed herself in the great amount of work which still remained, abandoning temporarily her own research project. Moreover, it was the depth and breadth of her knowledge of Ban Chiang and her expertise in the organization of this exhibition that became truly invaluable. The central essay in the catalogue, drawing from the work of Dr. Gorman, is hers.

The following staff members of The University Museum have been instrumental in this project's success, and our heartfelt thanks go to: Dr. Robert Dyson, Director of The University Museum for his overall support and faith in the exhibition; Dr. Gregory Possehl, Head of the Ban Chiang Committee; Lisa Lyons for her valuable information and moral support; Deborah Kramer for her assistance in the early planning stages; Deborah Wong and John Hastings for their organization of the data; Cheryl Applebaum for her assistance with the catalogue; Dr. Tamara Stech, Dr. Vincent Piggott, and Surapol Natapintu for their review of the metallurgy; Steward Fleming of the MASCA lab for facilitating analysis of exhibit objects; Virginia Green and her staff for superb conservation work; Caroline Stuckert and her staff for myriad and painstaking registrarial tasks; Theresa Nagel for assistance with insurance matters; Phoebe Resnik for public relations; and Carroll Sheppard in the development office.

From SITES' perspective, the following people deserve special mention, although many individuals have contributed their talents to this project: Peggy Loar, Director of SITES, for her unflagging enthusiasm in the face of early difficulties; Dennis Gould, former Director of SITES, for the initial commitment to the exhibition; Jim Mahoney for his design of the exhibition; Karen Fort for patient editing of the exhibition script; Walter Sorrell and the entire model shop staff; Ken Clevinger and his staff in the cabinet shop; John Widener for his attention to minute detail; Tamsen Fuller and Catherine Valentour for exacting conservation of objects in the exhibition; Victor Banks for writing and photography; Lothar Witteborg for his conceptual assistance in the exhibition's early stages; Nongpoth Sternstein for translation of the exhibition script from English to Thai; Mary Sheridan and Janet Freund for registrarial support; Eileen Harakal for public relations; Andrea Stevens for coordination of the poster and the catalogue; Antonio Diez for his assistance with the financial aspects of this project; Jeffrey Stann for help in fundraising; and Nelson Stephens, now retired from USIA, for his continual aid at the American Embassy in Bangkok.

Lastly, but very importantly, I would like to thank His Excellency Prok Amaranand, Ambassador to the United States from Thailand, and his competent and willing staff who made so many aspects of this project easier and, indeed, possible to accomplish.

Martha M. Cappelletti
Exhibition Coordinator
SITES

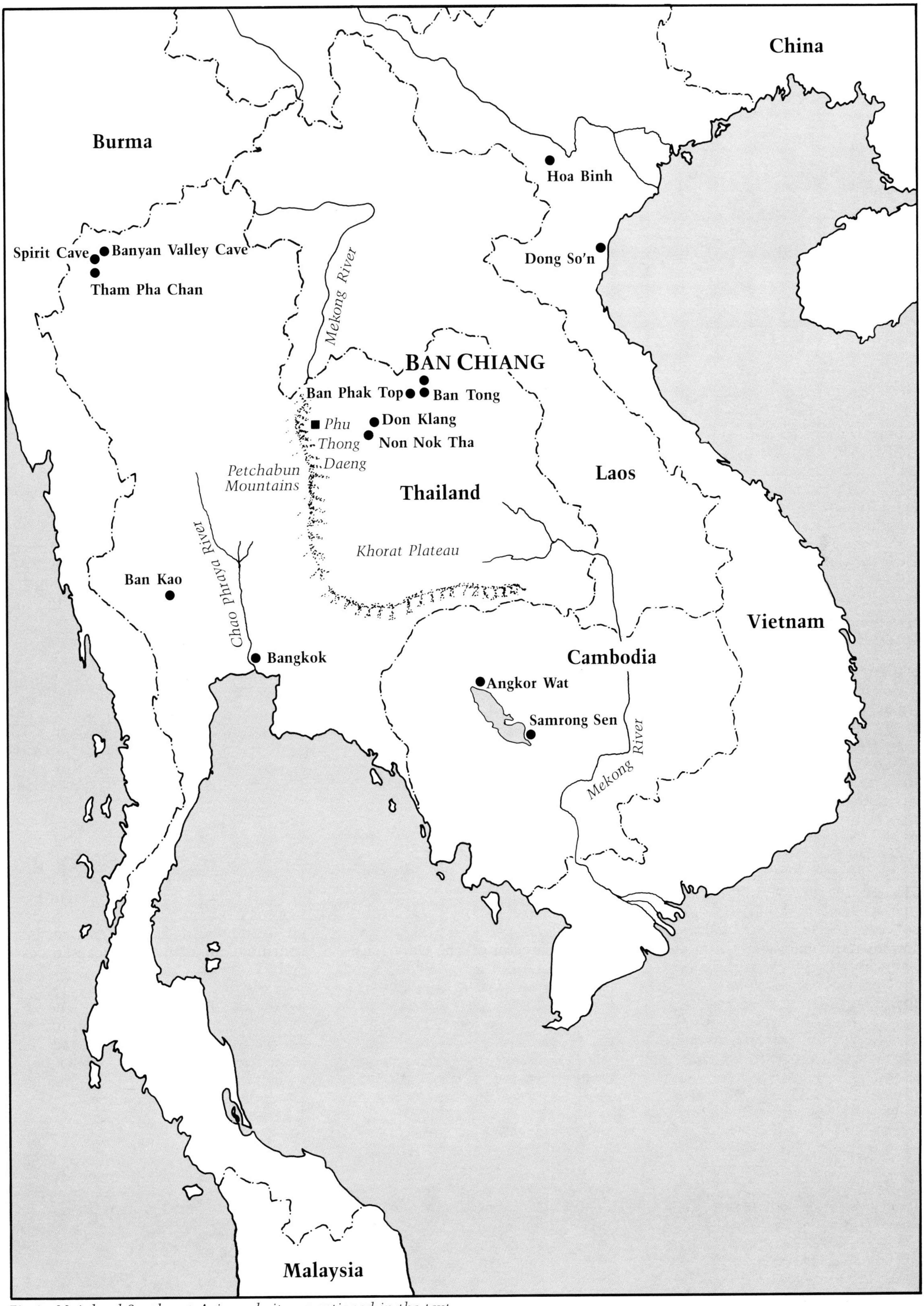

Fig. 1 Mainland Southeast Asia and sites mentioned in the text.

INTRODUCTION

by
Pisit
Charoenwongsa

Understanding a country as complex as Thailand is not easy. It requires some knowledge both of the past and the present—a comprehension of all the changes and forces that have given this country a civilization unique in its cultural and physical setting. It is unfortunate that the public and scholars alike have tended to accept oversimplified images and cliches about the people and society of Thailand without realizing that such judgments often lack an empirical basis. The fact that some scholars continue to present unsupported information about Thailand suggests either a lack of critical evaluation of scientific literature among scholars or a tendency to generalize among many who have researched and written about Thailand.

Archaeological data remains incomplete, and any reconstruction of Thailand's past inevitably involves some degree of speculation. According to noted British archaeologist Stuart Piggott, "We interpret the evidence in terms of our own intellectual make-up, conditioned as it is by the period and culture within which we were brought up, our social and religious background, our current presumptions and presuppositions, and our age and status." I hope in this essay to approach information about Thailand's past and present from an objective yet informed perspective and to present this little-known country in a clearer, more accurate light.

Pisit Charoenwongsa is head of the Research Section of the Archaeology Division, Fine Arts Department of Thailand, and was co-director of the Northeast Thailand Archaeological Project excavations at Ban Chiang.

A Country Called Thailand

Facts about Thailand are necessary in any introduction to the country, known in the West at least as early as the 16th century, due to a widespread lack of awareness about the country and its change of names from Thailand to Siam and back again. This misinformation about Thailand extends to scholars as well, as I discovered one evening at The University Museum, University of Pennsylvania. At the end of a talk on Ban Chiang I gave there in 1975, a member of the audience confessed to me: "I hadn't realized that Taiwan had a site that fascinating." In addition to this problem of mistaken identity, the variety of names by which Thailand is known has also caused some degree of uncertainty in the public mind. Names which Westerners use interchangeably with Thailand include Sarnau, Xarnau, Sion, Ciama, Siam, Ansean, and even Asia. The Thai or Tai call the country the vernacular name, Muang Tai, Land of the Tai, or literally "Land of the Free." During the reign of King Mongkut in 1856, the region was known as Sayam or Siam until 1939, when the government issued its official English name as Thailand. The name was changed back to Siam in 1945 for political reasons, and Thailand was again revived in 1949.

Fig. 2. Rice paddy land adjacent to the village of Ban Chiang during the dry season. (Photo by Joyce C. White.)

Fig. 3. Non Nok Tha, northeast Thailand. Joint excavation by the Thai Fine Arts Department and the University of Hawaii in 1966 and 1968 produced evidence for an early Bronze Age in Southeast Asia.

Land and People

Westerners, or "farangs," view the shape of Thailand as the head of an elephant with its trunk pointing to the south. To the Thai people, however, the map of Thailand resembles the shape of an axe or a water scoop with which they were familiar thousands of years before they undertook modern agriculture. This axe-shaped country has an area of 513,000 kilometers, roughly equivalent to the size of France, Spain, or the state of California, extending from the latitude 5°37′ to 20°27′N and from the longitude 97°22′ to 105°37′E. Thailand's greatest length is 1,650 kilometers, its greatest breadth 800 kilometers, and it is bounded by the neighboring countries of Malaysia, Burma, Laos, and Cambodia, and by the Gulf of Thailand and the Andaman Sea.

Geologically, some structural areas can be distinguished. The northern region is characterized by a system of folded mountains, the northeast by the uplifting of the Khorat Plateau, and the central region by the Chao Phraya Basin. In recent geological time, the southern region, part of the Malay Peninsula, was forcibly tilted slightly to the northwest. The western region is also characterized by hills and a high mountain range continuing from the western part of the northern region. The southeastern region, though it has flood plains of marine origin, is also rather mountainous especially in the east.

Except for the Chao Phraya Basin, structural flood plains, though large, are extremely narrow. There are several main rivers forming a network that offers easy communication; their flood plains and low terraces provide the option of farming as a way of life. A hundred years ago, Bangkok was known as the Venice of the East because of its elaborate canal systems. As a tropical country, Thailand was, until recently, known essentially for its rich evergreen and deciduous forests. Now, many forests are much reduced due to unplanned expansion of agricultural lands, exploitation of lumber for building material, for illegal fuel, and of course, for export as a commodity. Upland forests no longer serve as climatic regulators or as soil and water conservators.

In general, Thailand has three seasons. The cool season, from November through February, corresponds to the northeast monsoon; in most parts of the country there is too little rainfall for agriculture during this season or the next. The hot season, from March to May, is dominated by hot winds and local storm systems that carry negligible rainfall. The rainy season lasts from May through October, corresponding to the southwest monsoon.

Thailand's population of forty-seven million people includes a variety of ethnic groups whose different cultures have been integrated harmoniously into one Thai culture. Each group has retained its identifiable regional characteristics and customs. Thailand has experienced less ethnic and racial discrimination than its many neighboring countries. Positioned centrally in Southeast Asia, Thailand has since prehistory hosted interregional movements and hence, fostered interdependence among different peoples. Acceptance of obvious differences among its own people is an outstanding feature of the cultural character of Thailand. It is thus disturbing to find the conception of Thailand among scholars is of a "loosely-structured society" (Evers 1969). If the society is that ambiguously defined, one may wonder what holds the people together, and how did they meld into a nation-state. In fact, this widespread but mistaken notion is derived from a comparative study with Japanese society, and combined with generalizations about the history of Southeast Asia, constitutes an inappropriate approach to serious research. Because different people have different histories and cultures, it is unwise and even dangerous to loosely compare various institutions to one another. Moreover, the above theory is a description of the Thai people as viewed by yet another research team and indicates a lack of appreciation of Southeast Asian society: "Thais are better emulators than creators; better students than teachers; they have been borrowers rather than bearers of culture. . . . From many sources at many times the Thais borrowed cultural elements and have integrated them into their existing system, adapting them to match traits of their own character" (Moore 1974:3).

Developments of Archaeology in Thailand

It is true that the past does not necessarily set a precedent or predict the shape of things to come. But the past can structure perceptions of the present and expectations of the future in the minds of policymakers. King Rama V (1868–1910) wrote about his predecessor's Royal Assignments in which "Borankadi" (literally "archaeology") was included as a subject to which the king attended during an odd hour during peaceful times. Archaeology in the king's sense covered everything "ancient," including archaeology, ethnography, history, literature, and traditions. In 1907, toward the end of his reign, he established the Archaeological Club, three years after the inception of the Siam Society, which promoted and encouraged the study of the arts and sciences of Thailand. This interest in national heritage, achievements, and artifacts was continued by successive monarchs, including the present king. It is interesting to note that the first national museum in Thailand, which celebrated its hundredth anniversary a few years ago, grew out of a royal collection housed in the Royal Grand Palace. Partly because of the encouragement and advice of His Majesty the King of Thailand, the site of Ban Chiang has become a multidisciplinary and multinational research program.

Yet as far as archaeology in the modern sense is concerned, interest among the Thai people seems to be

Fig. 4. Test excavation at Ban Chiang in 1972 by the Fine Arts Department of Thailand.

more toward restoration of ancient monuments which are to a great extent identified with their religion, predominantly Buddhism. Prehistory seems remote indeed; it bears no direct concern with the present-day inhabitants of Thailand.

The Thai word for prehistory is of English origin; it was first used by Prince Damrong in the letters to his daughter beginning in 1934. Information concerning the prehistoric population of present-day Thailand was first recorded by a Frenchman about seventy years ago concerning rock paintings discovered in the south. Only a handful of Europeans resided in Thailand, mainly in Bangkok, most were members of the Siam Society and wrote articles on archaeological finds from time to time in the society's journal. Some started collecting polished stone adzes and soon acquired a greater number than the Bangkok National Museum. There was no serious professional study of archaeology until 1931 when Fritz Sarasin attempted his reconnaissance and test excavations of cave sites in north and central Thailand, searching for traces of earlier periods. As the country lies geographically between China and Indonesia where fossils of early hominids were found, Dr. Davidson Black of the Peking University came during 1927–1928 to explore the possibility of northward migration of the pithecanthropus from or through Thailand to China, though no such evidence was ever found. There were still no trained prehistorians among the Thais at this time. In 1931 when Professor Pietre Vincent van Stein Callenfells, director of the National Museum in Java, wrote the secretary to the king offering to train Thai officials in the field of prehistory, the offer had to be refused because the country then faced an economic crisis. In 1947 the prehistory of Thailand made headlines because of the writings of H. R. van Heekeren, a Dutch archaeologist who had been captured by the Japanese during World War II, and who was one of the prisoners compelled to work on the construction of the Bangkok-Moulmein Railway. Van Heekeren found stone tools near Ban Kao on a river terrace and a number of polished stone adzes in neighboring areas that he believed belonged to the Paleolithic period. His reports were both scholarly and adventurous because of the strange circumstances surrounding his archaeological discoveries as a prisoner-of-war. One of his earliest reports appeared in an issue of the *Illustrated London News* in 1947, bearing the title "Stone Axes from the Railroad of Death."

The Council of National Culture met on March 4, 1953, to discuss the human skulls and stone implements recently discovered in a cave in Suratthani, Peninsular Thailand, and unanimously agreed on the importance of the finds to national heritage and toward the understanding of the history of mankind. Immediate study was postponed for lack of trained personnel. The council then recommended that the Thai Fine Arts Department be given responsibility for research and for training its staff to work in this new field of study. As a result, the Faculty of Archaeology, Silpakorn University, added prehistory to its curriculum in 1955.

At first, prehistoric information was received only through accidental discoveries and one or two preliminary surveys. Systematic research was unheard of until 1960, when a team of Danish specialists began working in Kanchanaburi in cooperation with Thai officials from the Fine Arts Department, who in turn gained considerable field experience. More familiarity with field work was gained by the Thais following subsequent joint expeditions with foreign colleagues: in 1963 with the University of Hawaii led by Wilhelm Solheim and in 1966–1967 with a British team directed by W. Watson of London University. Now working on their own, the Thais have continued to engage in joint projects with colleagues from foreign institutions. Present projects include those with The University Museum, University of Pennsylvania; The University of London's Institute of Archaeology; The University of Otago in New Zealand; the Art Gallery of South Australia; and the Maritime Department of the Western Australian Museum. Each year foreign students have been granted permission to participate in these projects in the hope that by working together we will be able to put together a better and more accurate image of Thailand's past.

The BAN CHIANG TRADITION

Artists and Innovators in Prehistoric Northeast Thailand

Joyce C. White

Across the undulating landscape of the northern Khorat Plateau, northeast Thailand, archaeologists are discovering prehistoric sites of an artistically distinctive and technologically precocious people. Known as the Ban Chiang cultural tradition after its most renowned site, these communities of early farmers began to settle this region around 4000 B.C. Their tradition flourished there for at least four thousand years, into the beginning of the Christian era. These dynamic societies with their early and advanced metallurgy were unknown prior to the late 1960s, and the discovery of such innovative communities in a region traditionally regarded as a cultural backwater of China and India took the archaeological world by surprise. Scientists are just beginning to unravel the prehistoric puzzle of where this tradition originated, what its nature was, how it came to be, and how far its influence reached. Thus our understanding of these ancient societies may be quite different ten or twenty years from what it is at this writing. Such is the nature of scientific inquiry.

Exhibition curator Joyce White studied under the late Dr. Chester Gorman in the Department of Anthropology, University of Pennsylvania. She worked on the analysis of Ban Chiang at The University Museum for over two years before conducting her own ecological research at Ban Chiang during 1979–1981.

Southeast Asia: The Unexpected Place

It is interesting to note that even in prehistoric times, the autochthonous peoples of Indochina seem to have been lacking in creative genius and showed little aptitude for making progress without stimulus from outside.
(Coedes 1966:13)

Neither south-east Asia, Indonesia nor the Philippines experienced a phase of technology fully comparable with the Bronze Age in certain parts of the Old World. Yet, while stone tools continued in general use into the Christian era, a certain number of bronze artifacts, named after the rich settlement and cemetery of Dong So'n in northern Annam [northern Vietnam], found their way over these territories during the latter half of the first millennium B.C. and in the richer graves of Annam these were sometimes accompanied by objects made of iron.
(Clark 1971:238)

Since the publication of these statements, excavations in Northeast Thailand have revolutionized this traditional view of prehistoric Southeast Asia, and of the emergence of metallurgy in particular. In an area where no authentic Bronze Age was thought to have occurred, a distinct period during which bronze was the only metal widely used is now recognized to have preceded the appearance of iron. The recovery of implements for metal casting as well as technological residues such as spillage from filling molds shows that these bronze items did not merely find their way into the region from distant lands, but were made by local metalsmiths. Moreover, the date for the first appearance of metals, which Grahame Clark suggests is after 500 B.C., has been pushed back possibly two thousand years into the third millennium. This places the Southeast Asian Bronze Age at a time at least contemporaneous with that of northern China. The repercussions of these unexpected discoveries for theories concerning cultural development in Asia may take years to work out as future prehistoric research seeks to resolve the implications of recent excavations in northeast Thailand.

At the time that culture historians Georges Coedes and Clark made these statements expressing a cultural stagnation in Southeast Asia since antiquity, the prehistory of the region was in actuality a *terra incognita:* virtually no stratigraphic excavations had been undertaken using scientific methods of dating. The attention of those archaeologists interested in tracing the origins of Asian civilizations were focused on the conspicuous and imposing remains of the ancient cities and monuments of Mesopotamia, Egypt, India, and northern China. The ruins of Angkor Wat and other early city-states of Indochina were evidently later than and

Fig. 5. *Tham Pha Chan, northern Thailand, a Hoabinhian cave site excavated by Chester Gorman in the early 1970s.*

Fig. 6. *Spirit Cave, northern Thailand. Excavations here by Chester Gorman in the late 1960s and early 1970s uncovered Hoabinhian stone tools in association with possible evidence for incipient plant cultivation.*

derived from Indian and Chinese states. The dearth of serious archaeological investigation in Southeast Asia was due to, at least in part, the impression that the prehistoric material culture was probably based on organic materials that would have decomposed long ago in the steamy tropics. This prevailing opinion that archaeology in Southeast Asia would be unlikely to yield insights into the course of human development, leads one to wonder why any archaeologist would choose to dig in that area of the world. There were, however, indications from nonarchaeological sources that the prehistory of the region had far-reaching significance. Botanical data in particular suggested that prehistoric Southeast Asia was a region of autochthonous vitality and innovation, and that it spawned a distinctive way of life that had profound impact far beyond its centers of origin.

Since the nineteenth century a few scholars interested in the origins of cultivated plants have suggested that tropical East Asia was a likely place for early plant domestication (de Candolle 1883; Vavilov 1926; Darlington 1963; Li 1970). Geographers have proposed that plants such as rice, yams, taro, sugarcane, bananas, and many others now cultivated widely throughout the Indo-Pacific region were originally planted from wild progenitors indigenous to Southeast Asia. Carl Sauer (1952) even suggested that conditions in Southeast Asia were so favorable that this region might have witnessed the earliest development of agriculture. Without excavated and dated archaeological evidence for early agricultural societies, however, these suggestions remained untested hypotheses at best. Minority opinions were, of course, not taken seriously.

Not until the latter half of the 1960s did maverick archaeologists like Wilhelm Solheim of the University of Hawaii and his students Chester Gorman and Donn Bayard begin to seek evidence for ancient societies which might have undertaken early agricultural experiments. Opportunity arose to conduct salvage archaeology in Thailand in areas to be flooded by dams along the Mekong River and its tributaries. During a survey of the planned Nam Phong reservoir in Khon Kaen province, Gorman found an unpretentious but promising mound near Ban Na Di, Tambon Ban Khok, Phu-Wiang district. This site was subsequently excavated over two seasons, by Solheim, Hamilton Parker, and Bayard in 1966, and again by Bayard in 1968. The site, now known as Non Nok Tha, produced the first signs of an unexpectedly early bronze technology (Solheim 1971).

While the lowland site of Non Nok Tha was being excavated, Chester Gorman went to northwest Thailand to investigate Stone Age occupation of the uplands for his doctoral research. He discovered and excavated Spirit Cave which revealed occupation by Stone Age peoples back to about 10,000 B.C. The flaked stone tool tradition uncovered at Spirit Cave is known as the Hoabinhian, a technology prevalent in Southeast Asia in prehistoric times. The most significant discoveries at Spirit Cave, however, were the remains of plants suggestive of incipient cultivation (Gorman 1969, 1970). Although still controversial, these initial discoveries by Solheim and his students were to bring Southeast Asian prehistory from obscurity to world attention. These and subsequent excavations in Southeast Asia are challenging and transmuting orthodox theories on the origins and development of Asian civilizations.

Archaeological Exploration in Thailand, 1965–1973

So little was known about the prehistory of Southeast Asia in 1965 that whatever Wilhelm Solheim and his students brought to light was bound to defy expectations. The hunting and gathering substratum of the region known as the Hoabinhian had been defined in the 1920s when Madame Colani excavated cave sites in northern Vietnam (Colani 1927). The characteristic artifact of the Hoabinhian was a river cobble flaked along one side, often referred to as a "Sumatralith." A wide variety of associated animal bones from deer, wild pig, primates, rats, and other mammals, as well as mollusks and fish, indicated that a broad spectrum hunting strategy was employed. Since the species are still extant, it was surmised that the Hoabinhian people lived after the major faunal extinctions of the late Pleistocene, hence during the Holocene period. This strategy of using fauna to date sites was common before the radiocarbon method was developed in the 1950s.

Over the years assorted coastal and riverine shell middens and upland limestone rock shelters with similar stone tool assemblages were excavated from southern China to the Malay Peninsula and west to Burma. Claims for Hoabinhian sites were also made for Borneo, the Philippines, and even Australia (Clark 1971:233; Hayden 1977). The widespread and seemingly crude stone tool technology of the Hoabinhian existed at a time when European stone tool knapping had virtually reached the status of a fine art. Southeast Asia seemed at a rather backward cultural level, even "retarded" (Clark and Piggott 1965:49) in comparison. Thus, prior to the 1970s, the Hoabinhian hunter-gatherers were hardly considered likely ancestors of the pioneering lowland agriculturalists at places like Ban Chiang.

Modern scientific excavations of Hoabinhian sites since 1965, particularly those of Chester Gorman's in the remote hills of northern Thailand, have changed the perception of Southeast Asian hunter-gatherers from poky primitives to lively experimenters with plant cultivation, forerunners of lowland agriculturalists (Glover 1977). In view of the scarcity of flint and obsidian for the region, the "crude" unifacially flaked pebble technology

Fig. 7. Banyan Valley Cave, northern Thailand, a Hoabinhian cave site excavated by Chester Gorman in the early 1970s.

now seems to be the most efficient use of available raw materials (an "appropriate technology") rather than a sign of cultural retardation (White and Gorman 1979). It is also probably true that bamboo and other woods were used for many Hoabinhian tools. Still, the plants Gorman found are the most interesting and controversial part of this story.

The floral remains from the three Hoabinhian sites of Spirit Cave, Tham Pha Chan, and Banyan Valley Cave were studied by Douglas Yen (1977). Although the identifications and interpretation of these plant remains have been controversial, when viewed as a whole they indicate an interest in a wide variety of plant species, several of which became common garden varieties in the region by later times (Glover 1977:158). Some species such as *Areca* (betel nut) and *Lagenaria* (bottle gourd) are not now found in a wild state in the region, and hence may have been brought in from elsewhere. Others, such as *Trichosanthes* and *Momordica* (members of the squash family), are not edible when the fruit is fully mature, and the seeds hard. Yet, since they were identified from both carbonized and uncarbonized seeds, it seems that they were not incidentally discarded as a by-product of eating, but rather arrived in the cave for some other reason. One possibility is that the seeds were set aside for planting. Pending further recovery of plants from Hoabinhian contexts, Gorman's (1969) tentative conclusion that the assemblage of botanical remains from Spirit Cave "suggests economic development beyond simple food-gathering" seems justified.

On the lowlands of Northeast Thailand, the excavations of Non Nok Tha were producing even more startling indications of cultural sophistication in prehistoric times. At this mortuary site archaeologists unearthed socketed bronze axes and bronze bracelets plus sandstone molds and clay crucibles without any associated iron artifacts (Solheim 1971). Thus it appeared that the bronzes were locally made and that the technology preceded the use of iron. Stratigraphically the lowest metal artifact was a highly unusual item of enigmatic function found on the rib cage of a middle-aged male. This unique artifact (Fig. 42, cat. no. 11) was nicknamed WOST for World's Oldest Socketed Tool. It consisted almost entirely of a deep socket with an unusual shape: one surface is curved, but the opposing side is faceted into three planes. There is a short bladelike extension with a groove along the edge. Such a shape may have been used as a digging stick tip. Pending analyses in progress as of this writing, it appears that WOST may be unalloyed copper, the only copper artifact yet excavated from the early Bronze Age sites of northeast Thailand (Bayard 1972).

Actually these findings of bronzes and bronze-making implements were not unprecedented. Such items have been reported from haphazard excavations and stray findings all over mainland Southeast Asia for more than one hundred years. The Cambodian site of Samrong Sen excavated during the late 1800s produced bronze artifacts in association with polished stone. Since then socketed bronze axes, bangles, bells, fishhooks, spearheads, as well as axe molds and crucibles, have turned up in Thailand, Laos, Malaysia, Vietnam, and Indonesia (see reviews by van Heekeren 1958; Charoenwongsa 1978; Saurin and Carbonnel 1974). Without clear stratigraphic contexts and chronometric dates (absolute dates by radiocarbon or other methods), these finds had been interpreted according to traditional preconceptions. Thus a site containing both bronze and iron artifacts would be considered an Iron Age site regardless of the stratigraphic relationships among the objects. A site containing bronze associated with polished stone might be labeled a "late" Neolithic community which had had contact with an outside bronze-using people, ultimately the Dongson culture of Vietnam, traditionally considered the first Bronze Age people of Southeast Asia. This

Fig. 8. Looting at a Ban Chiang related site.

Fig. 9. Painted red-on-white pot (cat. no. 149). Painted pottery similar to this pot first drew the attention of both scholars and laymen to the site of Ban Chiang.

Fig. 10. Bronze bangles encircling a child's forearm (cat. no. 165). This object was brought from Thailand to the United States in the early 1970s and donated to The University Museum.

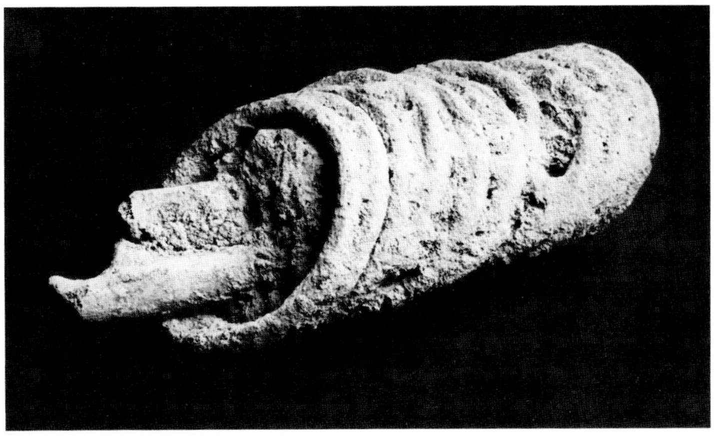

culture was first defined by material discovered in the 1920s at the site of Dong So'n in the Than-hoa province of northern Vietnam. It was characterized by spectacular bronze drums which were presumably found in association with iron. This association led to the assumption that both bronze and iron were introduced together from external sources. Basing his arguments largely on the comparison of decorative motifs, Heine Geldern (1951; 1954) traced the origins of the Dongson to eastern Europe. By means of coins and other evidence scholars cross-dated the culture to the late Chou and Han dynasties, that is, about the mid-first millennium B.C. (Pearson 1962:42). Whatever the source, the presence of bronze in prehistoric Southeast Asian contexts has traditionally been interpreted as a late and derivative technology. That the prehistoric bronzes may represent a distinctive technology indigenous to Southeast Asia was not seriously proposed until the initiation of modern archaeological research strategies at Non Nok Tha.

When the chronometric dates came back from the laboratory, the excavators of Non Nok Tha received a surprise greater than the mere discovery of bronze. These dates indicated that the earliest metals were much older than the Dongson culture. In fact the earliest Non Nok Tha metals appeared to be older than 2300 B.C., possibly even older than 3000 B.C. (Solheim 1968, 1971). Such antiquity, if corroborated, would not only challenge the role of Southeast Asia as a passive receptor of cultural developments from the outside but would even challenge the primacy of ancient metallurgy in accepted centers of innovation in the Near East, China, and India.

However, before such revolutionary ideas could be evaluated, much meticulous archaeological research remained to be done. Considerable controversy surrounded the interpretation of the Non Nok Tha chronology, not unexpected in the first excavation in an archaeologically unknown region, especially if the interpretation defied cherished notions. Contradictions in the dates (Bayard 1979) and difficulties in the interpretation of the chronology of four thousand years of intercutting burials crammed into one and one-half meters of deposit prevented the presentation of an irrefutable argument. Archaeologists expect corroborating evidence from other sites—a regional sequence—which demonstrates that a phenomenon such as unexpectedly early bronze is not just an isolated fluke but a regional pattern. Other sites needed to be excavated, preferably ones with deeper and clearer stratigraphy.

During the 1960s, other, often less official, investigations were drawing attention to a village called Ban Chiang, located 130 kilometers to the northeast of Non Nok Tha in Udon Thani province. For years the villagers, while building houses or gardening, had been digging up curious painted pottery and these vessels had simply been thrown out, used to hold pig slop, or kept for good luck. In 1960 a Thai Fine Arts Department officer inspected the site, but there was little official interest at that time in the archaeology of the pre-Buddhist periods. Thus, non-archaeologists were largely responsible for the early notoriety of Ban Chiang.

In 1966 Stephen Young, then a junior at Harvard University and the son of the United States ambassador to Thailand, visited Ban Chiang in the course of sociological research. One day while walking down a village road, he fell over the root of a kapok tree and came face-to-face with a hard round circle emerging from the ground—the rim of a pot. Looking about, he saw that these pot rims were eroding out all along the road, and he realized he was standing on an archaeological site. Since the sherds were unglazed, he assumed that they were quite old. Young brought samples back to Bangkok and showed them to officials at the Thai Fine Arts Department and to his hostess, Princess Chumbhot of Nagor Svarga, a wealthy, titled philanthropist and collector of Thai antiquities. When Elizabeth Lyons, then a fine arts consultant for the United States State Department, learned of the unusual pottery she arranged to have sample sherds sent to the Museum Applied Science Center for Archaeology (MASCA) at The University Museum, University of Pennsylvania for thermoluminescence dating, a newly developed method for dating fired pottery. In the meantime, the Thai Fine Arts Department conducted test excavations at the village in 1967 that uncovered stone tools and bronze as well as pottery. Foreigners and collectors from Bangkok began to come to Ban Chiang on a small scale to buy artifacts, particularly the unusual pot-

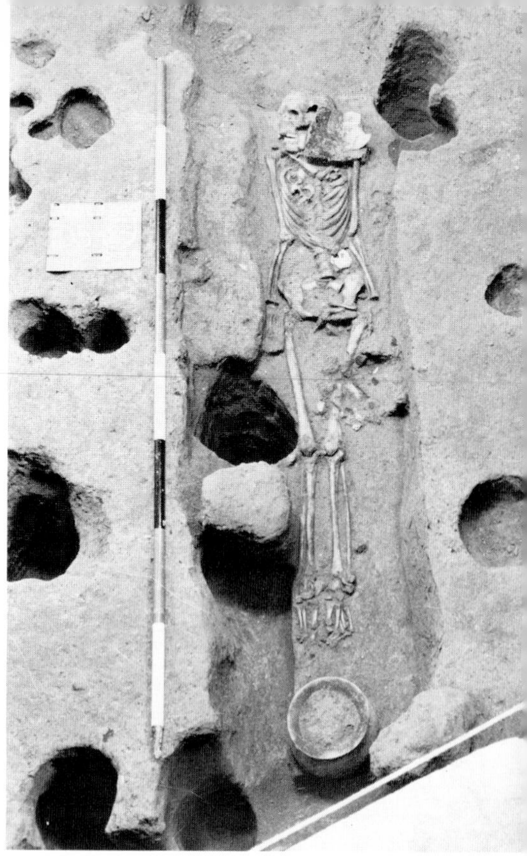

Fig. 11. Intercutting burials and postholes show that the site of Ban Chiang was used both for a cemetery and habitation.

tery painted with the red swirling designs.

When the results of the thermoluminescence dates were brought to the attention of Dr. Froelich Rainey, director of The University Museum, his first reaction was disbelief (Lyons and Rainey 1982): 4630 B.C. for a Bronze Age site in Southeast Asia was unheard of. He was aware, however, of the findings of Solheim and his students in Thailand, and of the hypotheses of Sauer and others that Southeast Asia might be an early hearth for the domestication of plants and animals. Serious investigation was certainly in order because the dates were merely intriguing until careful excavations produced corroborative evidence. The thermoluminescence runs were reported to the Thai Fine Arts Department in 1970.

Over the next two years these dates became known to the public, who in their naiveté concerning the complexities of archaeological research assumed that this meant that all of the Ban Chiang pots were six thousand years old. Ban Chiang was declared the new "cradle of civilization." Subsequent excavations were to reveal a more complicated ceramic chronology with the painted pottery dated to more recent times (fig. 18). Collecting pots became highly fashionable among Americans stationed at the air base in Udorn and among the wealthy of Bangkok. Villagers started to dig up their backyards to supply the shopping expeditions, and the pots went from meaningless curiosities to a source of income from which to buy medicine, send children to school, purchase televisions or even cars (Gorman 1981). Other Thais and foreigners became increasingly concerned over the massive looting and the resulting destruction at a site of potentially great significance. In 1972 the king sponsored an excavation at the village wat (temple), but this work was on the edge of the village mound and did not reveal the earliest levels. It did however bring to the attention of the villagers the importance of the ancient remains under their houses (van Esterik 1981; Charoenwongsa 1982). The Fine Arts Department conducted another excavation in the same year. These and other small-scale explorations of the site were simply too limited to deal with the size and complexity of Ban Chiang. A large-scale excavation employing careful stratigraphic controls and modern methods of retrieving minute ecological data was needed, and such an excavation would require the resources from international collaboration.

In September 1972 the undersecretary of state in the Ministry of Education of Thailand approached Elizabeth Lyons to investigate such a collaborative arrangement between a museum in the United States and the Thai Fine Arts Department. She immediately went to Fro Rainey, the director of The University Museum, who in turn visited Ban Chiang. Impressed with the condition, distinctiveness, and enormous volume of material emerging from looters' pits (Lyons and Rainey 1982), Rainey opened discussions with the Thai Fine Arts Department officials. Negotiations went fairly smoothly and The University Museum hired Chester Gorman (who at the time was completing excavations at cave sites in northern Thailand) to be the American co-director; Pisit Charoenwongsa was selected by the Fine Arts Department of Thailand as the Thai co-director. In 1974 the joint Northeast Thailand Archaeological Project (NETAP) was launched.

Excavations at Ban Chiang, 1974–1975.

When the archaeologists arrived at Ban Chiang in 1974 the immediate problem was where to dig. Unlike Non Nok Tha, the mound at Ban Chiang was entirely covered by a living village of tightly spaced houses. Furthermore, despite a law declared by the National Executive Council in 1972 against buying, selling, or transporting Ban Chiang antiquities, few parts of the mound remained undisturbed from looting. The first excavation in 1974 was located in the unlooted yard of a villager. During the second excavation season in 1975 the archaeologists sought an area closer to the center of the mound and selected the only undisturbed area they could find—down the center of a village road. Although more than 200 square meters were excavated to depths of up to 5 meters, archaeologists were able to sample only a small percentage of the original mound which measured approximately 500 by 1000 meters. Yet these limited excavations were conducted to retrieve a maximum amount of information and produced a wealth of material: more than 5000

Fig. 12. Site survey in northeast Thailand, 1975. Villagers are interviewed about archaeological finds in their area.

Fig. 13. Excavating an infant burial (BCES Burial 16). Exacting excavation methods were implemented by the NETAP.

Fig. 14. Red-on-buff painted pottery in situ *(BCES Burial 23/11). This style of pottery was found in the upper levels (Late Period) at Ban Chiang.*

Fig. 15. A scatter burial of the Middle Period (BCES Burial 40). Nine carinated pots were broken over this middle-aged man.

bags of sherds, 123 burials, more than 2000 other artifacts plus soil samples, animal bone, charcoal samples, and other items. Since the mound was considerably deeper than Non Nok Tha, there were high hopes that some of the chronological issues for the region might be resolved.

The NETAP had many goals beyond the careful excavation of one site. It sought to establish a long-term research program to gain a broad perspective on this dynamic prehistoric tradition of the Khorat Plateau (Gorman and Charoenwongsa 1976). It sought to upgrade standards for archaeological research in the region by introducing multidisciplinary research strategies and by training up-and-coming Thai archaeologists in the latest archaeological methods. During the first excavation season standardized procedures suitable for this type of mortuary site were developed to excavate and document with written, graphic, and photographic records all data recovered. All soils were sifted to retrieve every sherd, every scrap of animal bone. Sample deposits were processed through a flotation machine in which light materials such as seeds float and can be skimmed off. Specialists were brought in to expose the crew to methods and concerns of multidisciplinary research and to initiate long-term projects on human biology, animal and plant ecology, ancient metallurgy, and other topics (Gorman and Charoenwongsa 1976:16). Furthermore, systematic surveys were initiated to define the extent and pattern of ancient settlement in the region and to seek promising new sites for future excavations (Schauffler 1976; Penny 1982;. Kijngam, Higham, and Wiriyaromp 1980). Several of the Thai students went on to the University of Pennsylvania and the University of Otago in New Zealand to pursue graduate study after their experience in Ban Chiang (Charoenwongsa 1982), along with other young archaeologists from Burma, Indonesia, and the Philippines. The impact of the Ban Chiang project on the archaeology of Southeast Asia will be felt for years to come.

As at Non Nok Tha, the excavations at Ban Chiang uncovered primarily mortuary remains. One hundred twenty-three burials, most of which contained grave goods, were recovered from the two seasons of excavation. Postholes, probably from structures raised on piles, indicated that the mound had also been inhabited, but the wooden buildings have left little for the archaeologist to recover other than to document cylinders of earth somewhat darker than the surrounding deposit. Thus most of the data on the ancient society derive from burials—both a blessing and a handicap for the archaeologist. The practice of interring grave goods with bodies gives the archaeologist an unwitting gift since relatively intact artifacts are recovered, not just worn out or broken objects discarded in the trash. Moreover the argument for contemporaneity among all the items in a grave is clear and thus aids the archaeologist in determining stylistic sequences. On the other hand generalizing about an ancient culture on the basis of such a narrow range of behavior as funerary rites seems extraordinarily biased. The evidence from the activities of daily life is vastly underrepresented. The archaeologist must be constantly aware of the limitations of mortuary data, but still plunge on with the evidence that is available.

Over the course of the Ban Chiang excavations it became evident that the site was much deeper and richer than Non Nok Tha and in addition contained distinctive styles of ceramics and other artifacts. The red-painted pottery that captured public attention was literally the tip of the iceberg. It was found in only the uppermost layers underneath which were uncovered many additional levels of deposit and a great variety of other equally distinctive ceramics. Bronzes were also found in levels beneath the painted pottery, but because it tended to be scarce in the lower levels it was unclear if the first settlers had brought bronze. During

Fig. 16. White carinated pot reconstructed from a Middle Period scatter burial (cat. no. 44).

the 1974 excavations bronze was not found in the lowest graves.

During the 1975 excavation season, burial practices and ceramic styles not found in the first year showed how complex the history of this mound had been. Under the red-painted pottery archaeologists came down upon an unusual style of burial. Bodies were overlain by "sheets" of pottery sherds generally whitish in color (fig. 15). Were random sherds strewn over the body? Had whole pots been placed in the grave and then broken over the individuals? If so, how many pots and of what styles and sizes? The answers had to await reconstruction in the lab, but in order to be able to determine the placement of the sherds over the body special excavation strategies were undertaken. Each of these scatter burials was removed in three sections, each part assigned a separate series of bag numbers. Some of these scatter burials unexpectedly produced unusual bimetallic objects, including two spearpoints with iron blades and bronze hafts, plus a bronze bangle encircled by iron rings. One five-year-old child wore several iron bracelets. Under these scatter burials the soil changed from a reddish to a greyish color. Grave furnishing became simpler, bronze rarer. The intercutting of graves and postholes became highly complex and required intricate excavation in order to be able to decipher the sequence of events. Ironically some of the most important finds came at the very end of the second season as the baulks, the dirt from between the squares, were being excavated and the side walls were threatening to cave in. Following is an excerpt from Gorman's notes on the excavation of burial 76 at the bottom of baulk D6/D7.

Fig. 17. Excavating the baulks at the end of the 1975 excavation season at Ban Chiang.

September 16, 1975
While I was working on removing . . . (baulk) D6/D7 . . . we took a severe cave-in along the (East) sections of (squares) D5 and D6. Huge boulders of earth, large pots and sections of the fence came hurtling into our squares. Fortunately no-one was injured. The remaining weakened sections were too dangerous to work under, and two full rice houses just to the east of our excavation appeared to be in a very precarious position. In an effort to support these rice houses we began to backfill immediately. . . . In feature 5 of layer 27 baulk D6/D7 under the cranium we found a large piece of bronze—which is still there but must be lifted tomorrow (or today)—a bit dicey as the East section has loosened and is about 4 meters above; the smallness of the square D7 gives no room to run . . .

September 17, 1975
This morning I went down into D6/D7 to excavate the remainder of Burial 76 and the "bronze pin." As I went down it became obvious that the "bronze pin" was actually a socketed spearhead!! The burial was laid out flexed on its right side with its hands under its—rather between its knees; the spearhead was just at its knees, under the skull and next to the hands—we'll have to use . . . a person to draw the position since it was taken out quickly due to the possibility of another cave-in on the East Baulk . . . Interesting that our last and most dangerous to work burial would be exactly what we hoped for in the bottom layer.

At the end of the 1975 excavation season, eighteen tons of material recovered from the site were shipped to The University Museum for analysis. The human bone was sent to the University of Hawaii. The animal bone went to New Zealand to the University of Otago. Specialists began to pursue their individual studies, and the labor and time-consuming business of archaeological reconstruction and computerization began in the basement of The University Museum. (White et al. 1982; Schauffler 1979; Hastings 1982). Slowly the results have trickled out of the labs. Some preliminary observations based on field impressions were published in 1976 (Gorman and Charoenwongsa 1976) before the bulk of the laboratory analysis was undertaken. Revisions

Fig. 18 **Sequence of major burial and ceramic styles at Ban Chiang.**

Burial styles		*Characteristic Ceramics*
Late Period ca. 300 B.C.—A.D. 200 Supine burials with intact pottery placed over the body.	1 A.D. 1 B.C.	Red burnished pots. Red pots painted with red designs. Red on buff pottery.
Middle Period ca. 1000—300 B.C. Supine burials with funerary pottery shattered over the body.	300 B.C.	Carinated and carobel pots with thick red rims. White carinated pots. Incised and painted carinated pots.
Early Period ca. 3600—1000 B.C. Supine burials with pottery placed at the foot or the head of the grave. Flexed burials with and without grave goods. Infant jar burials.	1,000	Globular cordmarked pots with designs often incised and painted on the shoulder. Straight sided "beaker" and cordmarked wares; Cordmarked pots with tall necks.
	2,000	Infant burial jars and other pots with densely incised designs. Footed cordmarked wares often with incised designs on the shoulder.
	3,000	

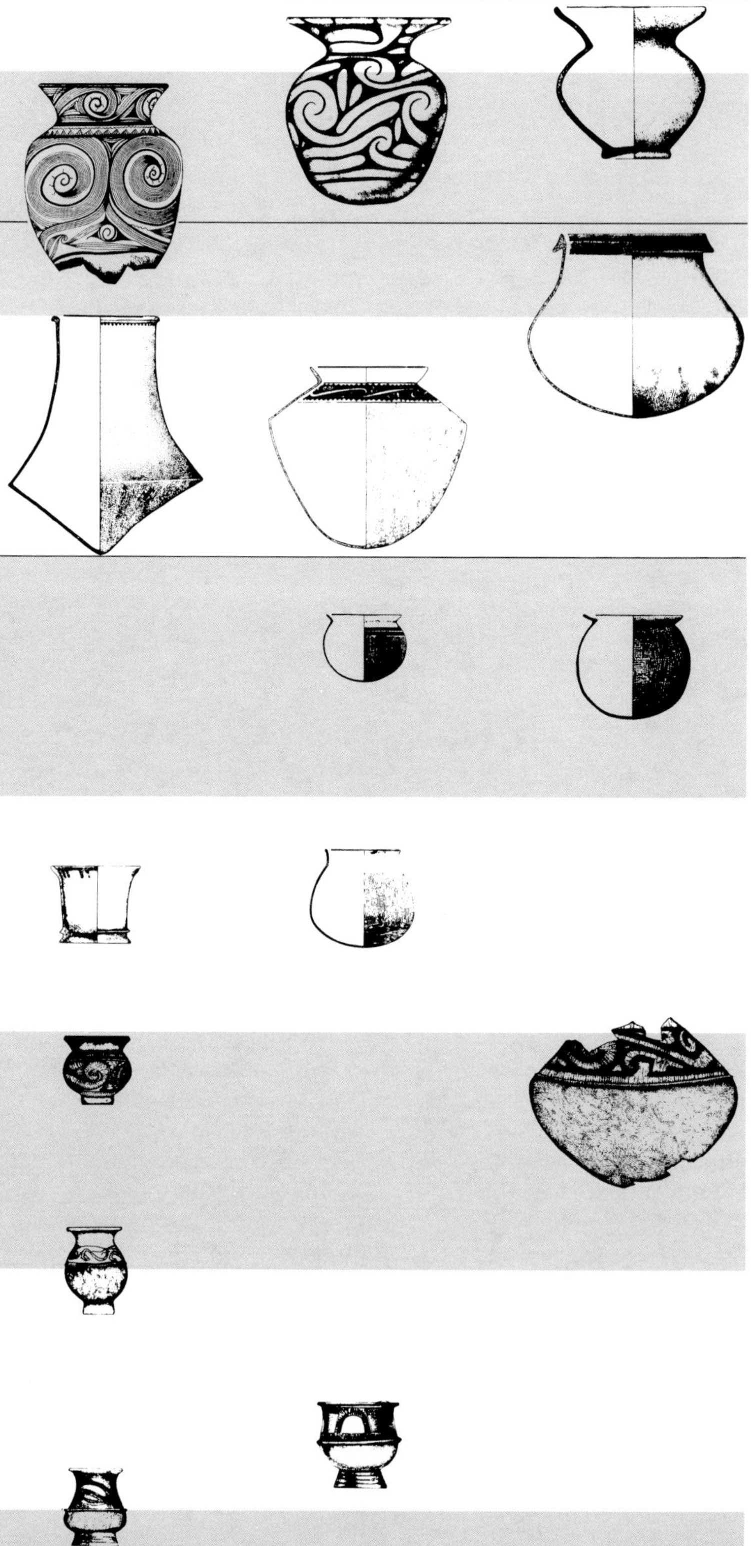

Fig. 19. Remnant of a dipterocarp forest near Ban Chiang. The large trees left standing when land is cleared for rice paddies provide clues to the natural vegetation. (Photo by Joyce C. White.)

Fig. 20. Fish trap in a stream near Ban Chiang. Traps provide an easy means to capture the fish abundantly available in modern-day northeastern Thailand. Similar traps may have been used by the prehistoric inhabitants, but the perishable nature of the materials makes it unlikely that any trace of the artifacts would survive in archaeological contexts. (Photo by Joyce C. White.)

in the chronology and typology since that time are reflected in this catalogue and will be more fully explicated in the forthcoming site report. Reports have also appeared on the human bone (Pietrusewsky 1978, 1981, 1982), fauna (Higham and Kijngam 1979, 1982; Higham et al. 1980; Higham et al. 1981), metals (Stech Wheeler and Maddin 1976), and rice (Yen 1982). Surveys, test excavations, and other field research (Schauffler 1976; Penny 1982; White 1982, i.p.; Kijngam, Higham, and Wiriyaromp 1980) have provided information on patterns of settlement and ecology. A picture of prehistoric life on the Khorat Plateau has begun to emerge.

The long grave sequence at Ban Chiang when dovetailed with other materials from the site and surrounding settlements can be used to develop an initial perception of what we have come to call the Ban Chiang cultural tradition. This encompasses four thousand years of prehistory in northeastern Thailand. What we see in this tradition is a fundamental continuity in ecology, aesthetics, and lifeways that is complemented with important changes and developments in technology. These developments never appear to have disrupted the ancient society, but rather were incorporated peacefully into its cultural fabric. The four thousand-year span can be subdivided into three major periods on the basis of soil stratigraphy, burial rites, and ceramic styles: Early Period, ca. 3600–1000 B.C.; Middle Period, ca. 1000–300 B.C.; and Late Period, ca. 300 B.C.–A.D.200. Within these periods ceramic styles changed, which allows further subdivision of the sequence into archaeological phases. If a ceramic style or other artifact type can be pinpointed to a time span within a period, this is indicated. However, a more thorough discussion of the phases at Ban Chiang will be forthcoming in scientific reports.

The Ban Chiang Cultural Tradition

Pioneering the Khorat in the 4th Millennium B.C.

From about 4000 B.C. settlers already adapted to simple village life on the Southeast Asian lowlands moved onto what is today the Khorat Plateau. These people settled in small groups along the middle reaches of tributaries of the Songkhram River which drains the northern part of the plateau, called the Sakon Nakon Basin. No signs have yet been found that this basin had been extensively occupied prior to this settlement.

Our understanding of those crucial first steps of adjusting to life on the Khorat Plateau is particularly hazy. The low density of sherdage from the early levels and the initial slow rate of soil buildup on the mound suggest that population density was low. There probably was considerable reliance on perishable organic materials for many of the material needs. Even today bamboo tubes can be substituted for pots for most purposes including cooking. Certain rice preparations, in fact, are roasted exclusively in bamboo tubes. The restricted area of the excavations also contributes to our limited view of the first settlers. Nevertheless the locations of the early settlements and the remains from the early period levels indicate the establishment of a number of trends that were to develop throughout the habitation as well as certain aspects of the ancient culture distinctive to the Early Period.

The first settlers most likely encountered a subtropical environment diverse in plant and animal resources. Northeast Thailand today lies in a tropical zone that receives all of its annual rainfall within about six

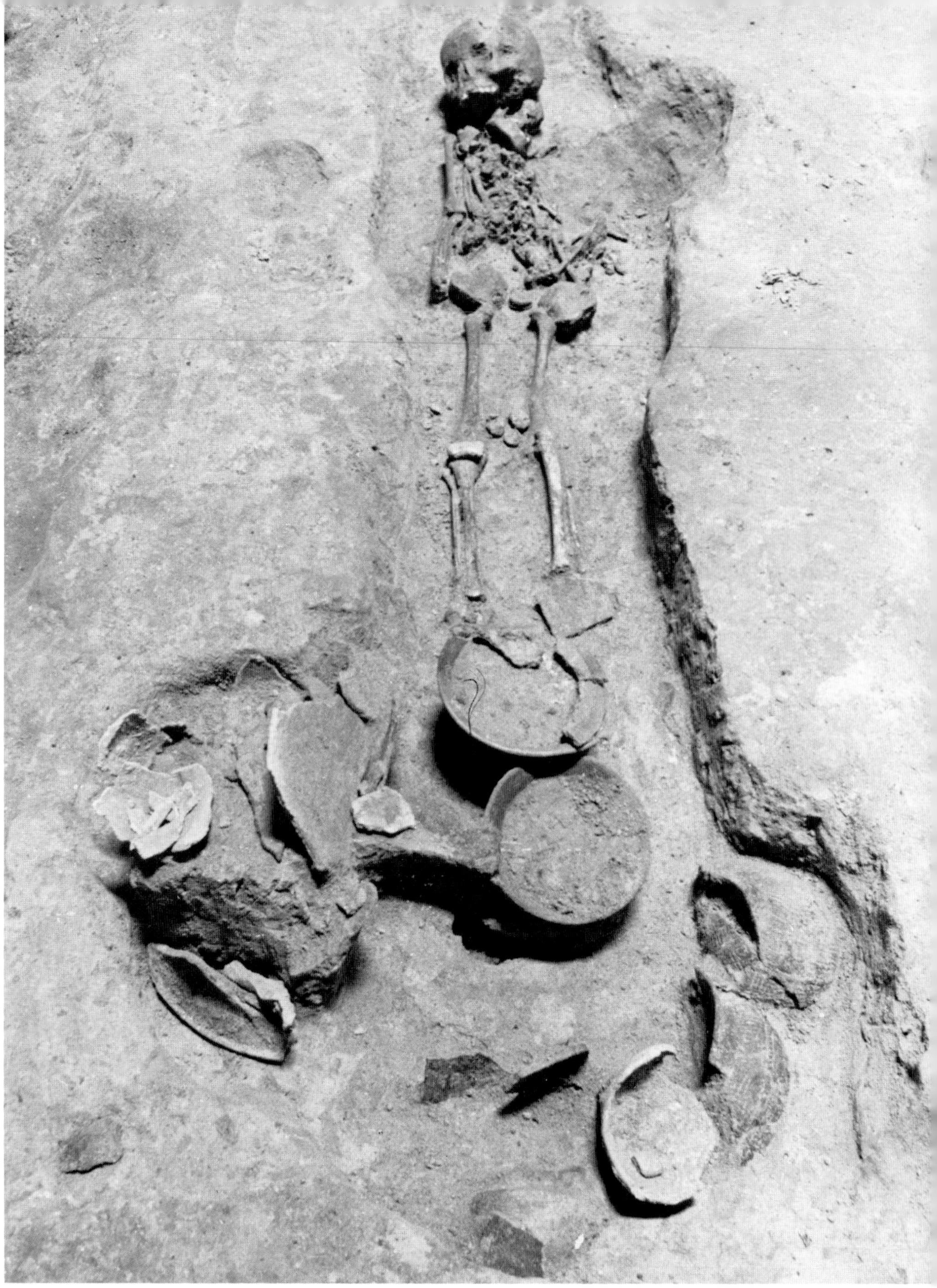

Fig. 22. An Early Period burial of a six-year-old child (BCES burial 52). Four pots were placed at the foot of the grave.

Fig. 21. House built on piles in the traditional manner in Ban Om Kaeo, a village near Ban Chiang. This house is constructed almost entirely of natural materials including a thatch roof, split bamboo flooring, and walls made from leaves sandwiched between woven bamboo frames. Rice is stored under the house in the cubicle made of woven bamboo sealed with dried mud. (Photo by Joyce C. White.)

months, May through October. Although the environment is lush green during the rains, in the dry season, November through April, the deciduous trees drop much of their foliage, lakes and marshes evaporate, the upper reaches of water courses run dry, and the water table drops. The study of ancient animal remains recovered in some of these early sites (Higham and Kijngam 1979) indicates that this seasonal distribution of rainfall dates back to the lowland settlement of this region. The plants and animals that inhabit this seasonal tropical environment have developed suitable behaviors and genetic adaptations to the annual fluctuation in water resources. Human societies in the present and presumably those of the past that have inhabited this region must also adjust their lifestyle to the ebb and flow of natural resources.

Across the gently rolling countryside of the Khorat Plateau one can still see remnants of the natural vegetation mosaic despite extensive agricultural development. The original vegetation would have ranged from open savannah-like, dry dipterocarp forests on the dryer soils to dense semi-evergreen vegetation on less rapidly drained areas. Modern-day inhabitants recognize the great diversity of their natural habitat and use this in their land-use strategy. Locations for different crops, even different varieties of rice, are carefully chosen and the locales where specific wild tubers, edible leaves, nuts, snails and other useful flora and fauna are well known. Wild relatives of many cultivated species including rice and several species of yams can, in fact, still be found in the Ban Chiang region, which lies within the theoretical zone for the domestication of many species adapted to the seasonal tropics (White 1982).

The broad spectrum of animal species known to the ancient inhabitants indicates that they likewise were aware of and exploited the environmental variation within range of their settlement (Higham and Kijngam 1979). Most of the animal species found in the prehistoric deposits have been known in the vicinity of Ban Chiang within the living memory of the elder inhabitants of the village. Studies of the prehistoric faunal remains of Ban Chiang and related sites show that the early inhabitants, in fact the inhabitants throughout the prehistoric occupation, made extensive use of the local wild animals and presumably exploited the wild flora as well. Hunted animals include forest dwelling species such as sambar deer, pangolin, and rhinoceros. Other hunted species such as rabbits, civets, frogs, mongoose, and grass turtle prefer more open vegetation. The ancient people also fished and col-

Fig. 23. A flexed burial of the Early Period (BCES burial 65).

Fig. 24. Infant jar burial of the Early Period at Ban Chiang (BC burial 40). Burial jar is catalogue number 28, a curvilinear incised pot.

lected various snails. Fish have been the most important source of protein in the area in recent times because of their natural abundance and ease of capture, but they were probably underrepresented in the faunal remains recovered from the sites because their small bones would tend to slip through the screens.

Although wild resources were clearly quite important to the prehistoric economy, the early settlers were not simple hunter-gatherers but brought with them practices indicative of considerable knowledge of a settled, food-producing way of life. Domesticated cattle, pigs, and chickens were raised from the earliest occupation. Domesticated dogs were also found in the early levels. They must have been brought into the area by the early settlers since the closest wild relative, the wolf, is not indigenous to Thailand (Higham et al. 1980). Water buffalo were notably absent from the earliest layers, but were well established by the Middle Period, ca. 1000 B.C. In addition to breeding domestic stock, the earliest inhabitants brought a settled village lifestyle that included building structures on piles or wooden stilts, making pottery, and probably practicing some simple form of rice cultivation. Part of the evidence for rice cultivation derives from impressions of rice found in the pottery at all levels of the site. Rice husks were probably purposely added to the pottery clay as a temper, a practice which is still used by potters in the Ban Chiang vicinity today. A study (Yen 1982) of the rice impressions in the ancient pottery suggests that the species may have been in the process of domestication by the ancient society. Since the rice was utilized prior to the appearance of water buffalo by the Middle Period, the nature of the Early Period rice cultivation system before the villagers could have had access to a buffalo-drawn plow is one of the most interesting research problems for the prehistory of the area.

The very location and style of settlement show that despite the prominent use of wild resources, a fundamental shift away from a mobile hunter-gatherer lifestyle had occurred. The commitment to building structures, maintaining domestic stock, making fragile and heavy ceramic vessels, and probably cultivating rice and other plants represents a social and economic strategy to plan for the longer term. This may have been necessitated by the seasonal fluctuation of resources, the scarcity of food during the dry season. Plant and animal cultivation are strategies for not only surviving this seasonal fluctuation, but also for exploiting it. The very same mechanisms that plants such as rice and yams use to store their nutrients over the long dry season in order to quickly send up shoots with the commencement of rains—that is large hard-coated seeds or fleshy tubers—are the same qualities that human societies have enhanced when they began to plant these species. Hence the roots of an agricultural lifestyle that prevails all over Southeast Asia and which has derivatives in regions far beyond may be examined in these prehistoric sites of the Khorat Plateau.

Early Period Burials, ca. 3600–1000 B.C.

Mortuary practices from the Early Period show considerable variation from individual to individual in the number, style, and placement of grave goods, and sometimes the positioning of the body. Adults and juveniles are most commonly interred in a stretched out or supine position, a

Fig. 25. The excavation of the Early Period Burial dubbed "Vulcan" (BC burial 23).

Fig. 26. Close-up of a contemporary pellet bow. Similar weapons might have been used to shoot pellets such as those found in Vulcan's grave.

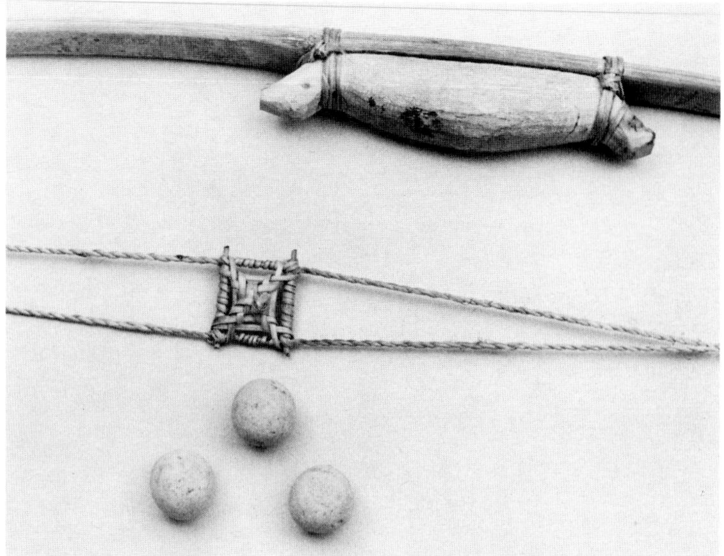

burial style which characterizes all three periods at Ban Chiang. During the Early Period one or more pots of various styles were placed toward the foot or the head of the body and occasionally jewelry or implements were also included. There are a few adults buried in a flexed or crouched position which is reminiscent of the style of burial used by Hoabinhian hunter-gatherers. However, these flexed burials are not found exclusively in the earliest burials, but seem to coexist with the supine burials until about 1600 B.C. One of the earliest flexed burials, that of a young man, contained one of the oldest bronze artifacts found in a grave—a socketed spearpoint (fig. 43, cat. no. 92). (The discovery of this burial is described in the previous section.) The tip of this spearpoint had been bent prior to interment, an interesting and early example of the practice of mutilating or "killing" grave goods. Purposeful destruction of grave goods is found in the Middle Period as well. Similar practices have been found in the recent excavation of Ban Don Ta Phet in Kanchanaburi province at a much later date (Glover 1980).

Infants received special treatment during the Early Period. Several jar burials were found containing human remains ranging in age from a seven-month-old fetus to a two-year-old child. Generally the remains were at most a few weeks old. This practice, together with the high proportion of infants, is peculiar to the Early Period,

Fig. 27. An elderly man making a pellet bow at Ban Om Kaeo, a village near Ban Chiang. (Photo by Joyce C. White.)

but the meaning of this distinctive treatment is not known. Some possibilities may be suggested for the seemingly high infant mortality. It may be an indication of a somewhat precarious existence, a result of an unreliable resource base during the early phases. On the other hand the society may have attempted to keep its population in balance with the resource base by using infanticide, a form of population control not unknown, particularly among nomadic groups. However, the prominence of this type of burial in the Early Period may be a peculiarity of archaeological sample bias; at later times infants could have been buried in another location not uncovered during the NETAP excavation. Whatever the reasons, both the practice of burying very young humans in jars and the relatively high proportion of infant burials are characteristic of the Early Period, and no jar burials were found in the Middle or Later periods during the Ban Chiang excavation.

One of the key patterns that archaeologists look for in burial sites is evidence of social distinctions recognized by the ancient society, since increasing social complexity is considered one of the hallmarks of the development of "civilization" out of simpler more egalitarian societies. Two Early Period burials, both dating to about 1500 B.C., have distinctive sets of grave goods which are suggestive of very early stages of social differentiation. One middle-aged male was nicknamed "Vulcan" by the excavators due to the prominence of bronze grave goods that included a socketed adze and four bangles. He was also buried with a pile of about thirty pellets to the right of his skull, and with a painted and incised pot at his feet (fig. 51). The pellets have been interpreted as projectiles for use with a pellet bow, a type of weapon with a split string and a tiny woven platform against which the pellet can be grasped (cat. no. 176). These bows were used in the Ban Chiang vicinity until about fifty years ago, and can still be made by a few old men (fig. 27).

Another burial of a younger male, dubbed "Nimrod," possessed a unique assemblage of bone artifacts (fig. 52,

Fig. 28. Incised and painted carinated pot reconstructed from a Middle Period scatter burial (cat. no. 42).

cat. nos. 126–129): two drilled tiger's teeth found at his neck as though they had been strung as pendants, a drilled "pin" interpreted as a hair pin since it was found adjacent to his skull, a spearhead and a carved antler of unknown function found alongside his left arm. The grave contents of both interments are not necessarily suggestive of unusual wealth or propertied status but rather hint more at special roles they may have played in the prehistoric society. Vulcan's grave goods seem primarily utilitarian, and Nimrod's were perhaps symbolic. A more precise meaning of these individuals to their society will probably never be known to us but we can sense that these men had acquired a revered status through some special contribution they made to their village, a first step toward social complexity.

Middle Period Burials, ca.1000–300 B.C.
The Middle Period was heralded by changes in funerary rites as well as new styles of ceramics and technological developments. In the 1975 excavations a clear change in soil color also separates the Early Period (greyish soil) from the Middle Period (reddish soil). Unlike funerary ceramics of the Early Period which, if found broken, were crushed in place from the pressure of the matrix, the funerary ceramics of the Middle Period were mostly found as sheets of broken sherds spread over and sometimes under the skeletons. The earlier burials of this type might have had just one large pot broken over the body (cat. nos. 37, 38), but subsequent burials might have contained nine to eleven large carinated pots, combinations of elegant white vessels and ruddy-toned wares with designs painted and incised on the shoulder (fig. 16, 28, cat. nos. 39–44). The horizontal orientation of the sherds indicates that the pots were broken

Fig. 29. A scatter burial during the later part of the Middle Period (BCES burial 12). The orientation of the sherds over the one-year-old child indicated that a grave had been dug for this individual, unlike other Middle Period scatter burials (cf. fig. 15.)

over the body while resting on a broad flat surface, not in a grave. Dirt might have been mounded over the individual. The exception was the grave of a one-year-old child who was found under broken sherdage from a total of seven pots. Some of these were carinated, but some had a distinctive globular shape (cat. no. 45); all had thick red-painted rims. This child from the late part of the Middle Period was clearly buried in a grave, as indicated by the vertical orientation of the sherds around the grave edge. Months of sorting, fitting, and glueing per scatter burial were required to piece together the pots from each sherd sheet.

As with the burial treatment of Nimrod, Vulcan, the jar burials, or really any burial, the ancient meaning of shattering the pots over the body is elusive. Yet the practice hints at a prosperous society willing to "throw away" a considerable investment of labor and resources required to make the large and elaborate funerary vessels. There are other indications that during the Middle Period village life in Ban Chiang had reached a stage of florescence. Bronze bangles not only became more common, but also stylistically more elaborate. Moreover, iron appears in both bangles and as blades with bronze hafts in bimetallic spearpoints. While very young infants are no longer found, young children were buried with a funerary style and grave goods commensurate with adult burials. Indeed, metal bangles are

Fig. 30. Skeleton of a one-year-old child with bronze anklets and bracelet (BCES burial 16, Middle Period). Bronze bangles were commonly found on the skeletons of children.

more commonly found with children than with adults although small sample size precludes firm conclusions.

What might lie behind this emergence of prosperity and seeming well-being of the Middle Period? One factor may have been the coalescence of the system of wet rice cultivation. Although water buffalo are absent from the earliest levels, by the Middle Period water buffalo appear to be firmly established at Ban Chiang (Higham and Kijngam 1979). Furthermore, studies of the forelimb bones indicate that the water buffalo were used for some sort of traction (Higham et al. 1981). While no iron ploughshares have been excavated, the presence of iron artifacts in Middle Period graves leaves open the possibility that an iron tipped plough might have existed. If so, all the fundamental pieces for the lowland wet rice agricultural system would have been in place at Ban Chiang by about 1000 B.C. This agricultural system had great potential productivity and may have formed a more reliable subsistence base than was possible with the earlier pre–plow cultivation.

Fig. 31. Baked clay figurine possibly depicting a water buffalo (cat. no. 48).

Fig. 32. A Late Period burial of a three-year-old child (BCES burial 8). Pots were placed intact over the body. Carved clay rollers were placed at the feet of this child.

Late Period Burials, ca. 300 B.C.–A.D. 200

Life at Ban Chiang continued to prosper during the Late Period judging from the range, diversity, and elaboration of the grave goods. The burial style returned to one of placing intact vessels in the grave—generally directly on top of the body. The funerary ceramics included the classic red-on-buff painted pottery, as well as other styles. Iron was used exclusively for tools which were placed in the graves of some males. Bronze at this time was used only for ornament. The most notable technological development was the appearance of a high tin-bronze of more than 20 percent tin requiring special metallurgical skills including hot working and quenching. This bronze was used to make wire necklaces—further evidence of a willingness to expend considerable investment of energy for nonutilitarian purposes. Similar concern for ornamental elaboration is notable in new items in the material culture inventory including elaborately carved ceramic rollers (cat. nos. 62–81) that might have been used for textile printing (van Esterik and Kress 1978), and glass beads (cat. nos. 90, 91). Interestingly, at Ban Chiang only graves of children contained beads, rollers, and the high tin wire necklaces. None of these items were excavated from adult graves. The placement of such special items with children hints that the children were held in high regard. Possibly their status and wealth were inherited from their parents. Further excavation at other sites of the Ban Chiang cultural tradition may clarify the pattern of social development in the region.

Fig. 33. Unprovenienced red-on-buff pot with deer (?) depicted at the base (cat no. 150).

Ban Chiang Ceramics: An Artistic and Technological Tradition

The excavations at Ban Chiang uncovered a previously unknown and aesthetically distinctive ceramic tradition stretching back nearly 4000 years beyond the red-on-buff pottery which gave the site its early renown. Known chiefly from pottery found in burials, the ceramics from even the lowest levels exhibit an elegance, sophistication, and attention to decorative detail that far exceeds mere utilitarian needs. The funerary wares clearly served as an art medium.

Although stylistic treatments can be discerned which are characteristic of delimited time spans, the ceramics as a whole are highly diverse, individualized, and resistant to simple categorization. This causes much frustration for the archaeologist who counts on standardized "types" to assist in deciphering chronology. There are, however, decorative treatments that characterize the tradition as a whole. In particular the freehand application of abstract designs can be found throughout the ceramic sequence. These designs, usually simple to complex curvilinear scrolls and spirals plus geometric motifs, may be incised as in some Early Period pots (e.g., cat. nos. 19, 23, 24, 28); incised and painted as is most often found in late Early Period and Middle Period pots (e.g., cat. nos. 34, 35, 37, 38, 40, 42); or painted only as in the classic red-on-buff wares of the Late Period pots (cat. nos. 54, 55, 56, 146–154). The intricate and precise composition of the design field which is well known for the red-on-buff pottery (van Esterik 1981) is equally remarkable in the incised wares of the Early Period (fig. 35). The rarity of depictions of humans, animals, or other natural forms is as characteristic of the Ban Chiang aesthetic as is the popularity of abstract designs. A few examples of painted representations of natural forms have been found on unprovenienced pots (fig. 33, 34, cat. nos. 152, 150, 147), but no examples were excavated by the NETAP.

In addition to their decorative continuity, the Ban Chiang ceramics exhibit a formal coherence throughout the sequence even though specific shapes have restricted time ranges. Rounded bases to which a foot has

Fig. 34. Detail of figure 33 showing a close-up of the possible deer rendering.

Fig. 35. Inked drawing of an Early Period incised pot illustrating the elaborate design (cat no. 24). (Drawing by Adriana Kulczycky.)

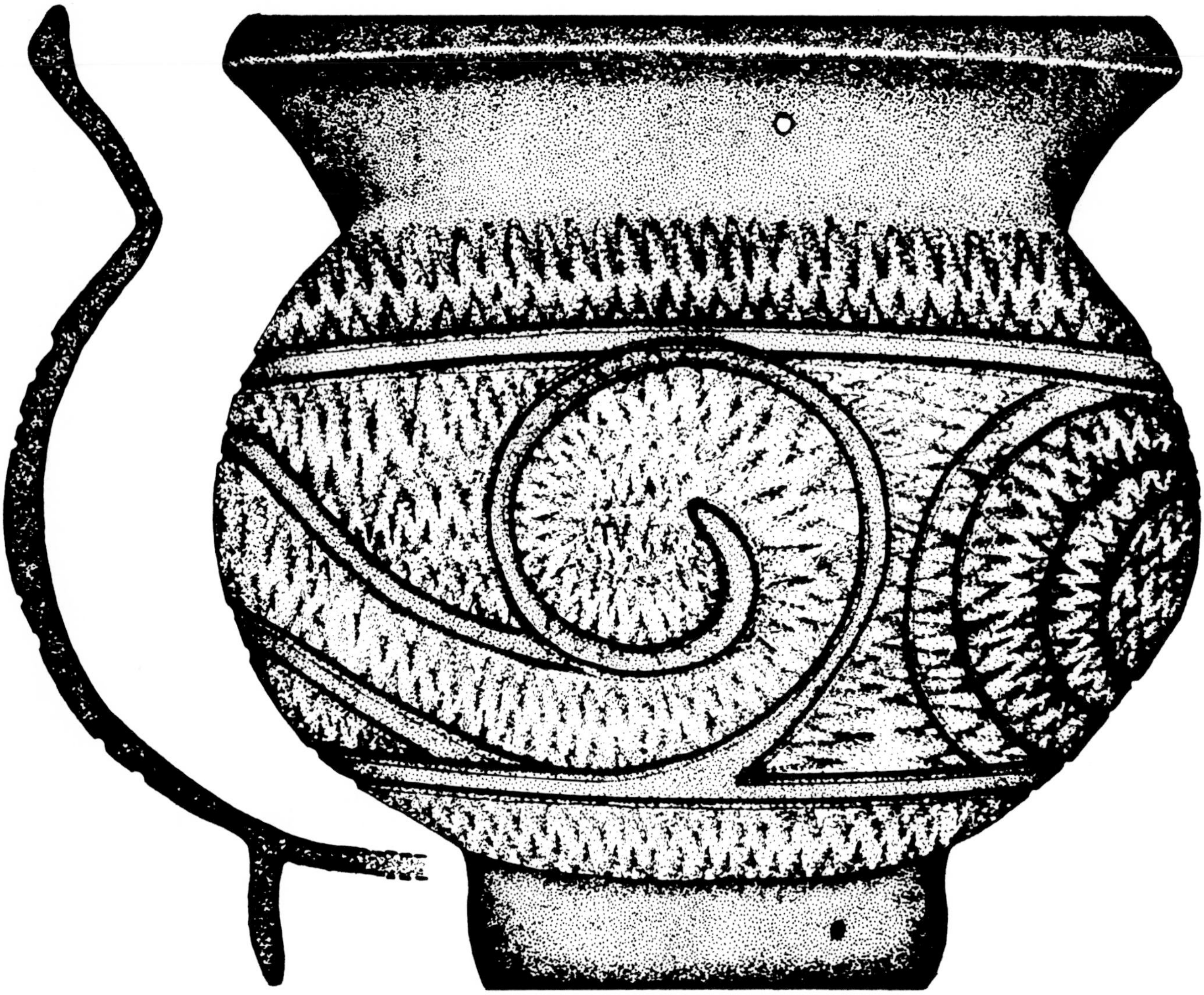

sometimes been added are characteristic, but handles, spouts, or other utilitarian modifications are rare. The range of shapes is in part a product of the manufacturing technology which employed the paddle and anvil technique in the construction of the vessels. This technique was widespread throughout prehistoric Southeast Asia and indeed is still used by potters in northeast Thailand today.

One variant of the paddle and anvil technique is used by contemporary potters to make water jars and cooking pots in the village of Ban Kham Oo, located about five kilometers north of Ban Chiang. Observation of these potters has given some appreciation for how the prehistoric pots might have been constructed, although the diversity of the ancient ceramics shows that the ancient potter used many additional techniques not presently employed. Contemporary potters collect clay from a meander in a local stream bed. A grog is made from a mixture of rice husks and clay which is shaped into balls, baked, ground, and finally sifted. The potter mixes the grog with more clay on a woven mat by kneading and stamping the two materials with her feet. Vessels are begun from lumps of the clay preparation by forming open-ended cylinders. The cylinder is placed on an upright log and the potter forms the rim first by grasping the top of the cylinder with a wet leaf and moving quickly and smoothly around the log. When the rim has been thus formed the potter holds the cylinder in her lap and beats the exterior with a wooden paddle while supporting the interior with a baked clay anvil (cat. nos. 179–181). The beating process closes the base of the cylinder and shapes the globular contour of the pot. If a foot is to be added, the pot is replaced rim down on the log and a second cylinder of clay is pinched and pressed onto the base. This is in turn smoothed and shaped using the same procedure employed in forming the rim. The only decoration that might be applied is a geometric pattern stamped onto the shoulder from a carved wooden paddle. Otherwise the pots are dried for about two days and then fired in the open for about 30 minutes on bamboo frames using rice straw as fuel.

While this contemporary example of the paddle and anvil technique illustrates the method possibly used to produce the rounded contours of many of the Ban Chiang pots, more impressive is the repetitive standardization of the contemporary pottery in comparison with the diversity and individuality of the forms, decorative treatments, and colors of the ancient ceramics. Of the many techniques employed by the ancient potter but not used in the area today, the most notable example is cordmarking. This surface treatment is found throughout the Ban Chiang ceramic sequence and

The Roots of Man

Scientists are constantly pushing back the frontiers of archeology and anthropology. Last week, researchers in Thailand and at the National Cancer Institute in Maryland were pondering theories that could produce a dramatic re-evaluation of one of science's oldest questions: the origin of man.

DAWN OF THE BRONZE AGE?

For archeologists, Southeast Asia has always been something of a cultural backwater—nothing to compare with Egypt, Greece or the lands once nurtured by the Tigris and Euphrates rivers. Then, just ten years ago, a vacationing Harvard student found some curiously painted pots in a road cut near the dusty village of Ban Chiang in northeast Thailand.

Today, scientists at Ban Chiang are working round the clock to keep ahead of looters. They are convinced that they have found the remnants of one of the most ancient centers of civilization yet unearthed—the dwelling place of a Bronze Age people whose metallurgy may eventually establish them as even more advanced than were the inhabitants of Mesopotamia 5,000 years ago. Just where these antique Asiatic people came from is a mystery. But from spearheads, pottery and other artifacts discovered in their burial mounds, there is no question that their civilization is at least as old as that of the Middle East.

The area of excavation covers a wide arc of Thailand's Khorat Plateau, extending for about 200 miles from the east to the southwest of Ban Chiang (map). Archeologists think that the region contains as many as 300 ancient burial mounds and habitations. Ban Chiang is the largest and deepest of the 60 sites located to date, and contains the remains of more than 15,000 individuals.

At first, most scientists were chary of the new finds, and even after the new technique called thermoluminescence* indicated the extraordinary date of 4,000 B.C. for some fragments, the experts thought that it was the method that had gone awry.

But when further dating confirmed the ages and new digging yielded a cornucopia of pots of different varieties, it became clear that Ban Chiang was an archeological treasure house. Two years ago, an international team headed by Chet Gorman of the University of Pennsylvania Museum and Pisit Charoenwongsa of the National Museum of Bangkok began a major dig in the area.

Thus far, the excavation has produced 18 tons of pottery, stone and metal items, 126 human skeletons, many animal fossils—and a picture of an extraordinarily sophisticated ancient society that occupied the region from about 3600 to 250

*Thermoluminescence gauges the age of pottery by heating fragments and measuring their radioactivity.

Ib Ohlsson

B.C. The prize item of the collection is a 5,600-year-old bronze spear point that is almost certainly the oldest artifact of this particular alloy ever found anywhere.

The major difference between the spear point and more ancient Mesopotamian bronze artifacts is the content of tin in association with copper. Middle East bronze older than 5,500 years inevitably consisted of copper and arsenic, because the Mesopotamians of the time had no ready source of tin. Written records indicate that they happened on a supply of the metal "from the east" somewhat before 3000 B.C. The Ban Chiang discovery thus raises the possibility that Thailand gave the Middle East its tin at least 2,000 years before any known contacts between these parts of the world.

Smelters: The ingenuity of the Ban Chiang civilization, which according to Gorman came to the area at least 7,000 years ago, did not end with bronze making. Its metallurgists were smelting iron before 1500 B.C., at the same time as the Hittites of Asia Minor, and its artists were fashioning painted pottery in many ways superior to contemporary Chinese art work. "I believe we have only begun to appreciate just how advanced these people were," said Gorman last week. "This was a very vibrant and sophisticated society. In terms of metallurgical skill, it seems to be unparalleled anywhere in the world." Gorman thinks that the people of Ban Chiang possessed all the skills, materials and social order necessary for urbanization—and he now plans to start looking for evidence of ancient cities in the area.

If the finds at Ban Chiang lead to the discovery of a still older society, archeologists may decide that Southeast Asia is a more fruitful area for research on ancient man than any place yet studied.

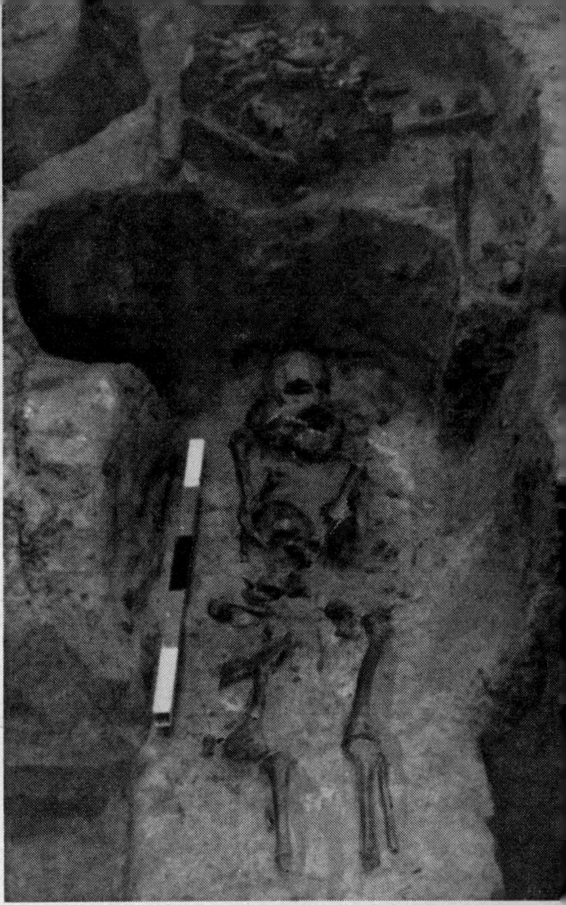

Grave at Ban Chiang: The tin connection

ASIAN GENESIS?

Where did mankind originate? Fossil studies by Richard Leakey and other anthropologists suggest that early man emerged in Africa more than 3 million years ago, but two virologists have now produced evidence for an Asian genesis of the human race.

Raoul E. Benveniste and George J. Todaro of the National Cancer Institute came up with the new theory after analyzing small lengths of DNA, the stuff of life, known as viral genes. The viral genes of modern man, they found, resemble those of Asian apes more closely than they do the viral genes of African primates. The researchers conclude in Nature magazine that man probably evolved from his nearest primate relatives about 14 million years ago in Asia. Not until 11 million years later, they suggest, did man establish himself in Africa.

So far, anthropologists have treated the new theory with restraint. "It's a single piece of evidence, and I'm not sure how much can be made of it," said Donald C. Johanson of the Cleveland Museum of Natural History, who has made extensive fossil finds in Ethiopia. "But I personally would not rule out Asia as the prime area for the beginning of man." Todaro and Benveniste meanwhile are furthering their laboratory studies, in hopes that they may also provide clues to man's susceptibility to cancer.

—PETER GWYNNE with STEPHEN G. MICHAUD in Philadelphia and bureau reports

By George F. Will

Taking a Ride With Ronnie

Ronald Reagan recently found himself in Detroit, in front of a spiffy audience, the Economic Club. With the insouciance that makes politicians do daring deeds with careless smiles, he praised the automobile. His words were well received, especially those deploring the yoke of government oppression under which the automobile industry labors. Then his listeners went home to cold stone slabs in Grosse Pointe dungeons, or wherever the oppressed lay their weary heads.

Reagan's Detroit message is worth pondering, and not just because one in ten American jobs is related to the manufacture, maintenance or operation of automobiles. His words display a troubling aspect of his brand of conservatism.

Reagan warned that "the automobile and the men and women who make it are under constant attack from Washington." The attackers are "elitists . . . some of whom seem obsessed with the need to substitute government control in place of individual decision making." He cited the Energy Policy and Conservation Act of 1975:

". . . It mandated gasoline mileage standards which by 1985 will have the effect of forcing Detroit to make some 80 to 90 per cent of its autombiles subcompacts or smaller . . . The bill regulates the marketplace, dictates to the consumer and, in the process, will make Detroit's unemployment problem worse than it already is. In fact, because it takes less manpower to make these small cars . . . the unrealistic fuel-use standards . . . would cost at least 200,000 Michigan workers their jobs . . ."

OFFENSIVE STANDARDS

Today the booming automobile industry does *not* resemble a patient etherized upon a table. The law that Reagan believes may etherize Detroit mandates a 50 per cent increase (based on the 1973 average) in fuel efficiency by 1980.

In 1973, the new-car average was 13.2 miles per gallon. The new law requires a 1980 average of 20 mpg. The industry's compliance will "produce" 2 million barrels of oil a day. That is like constructing another Alaska pipeline. The lash of the law, not market pressures, will accomplish this. And it makes economic sense. The cost to the industry of complying with the law will be passed on to car buyers. But that cost will be much less than the higher fuel costs consumers would have paid to operate the less economical cars which, but for the new law, Detroit would have produced.

The 1985 standards that offend Reagan require a 27.5 mpg new-car average. The standards petrify General Motors, which guesses that "85 per cent of all the new cars built in 1985 and after can be no heavier than today's Chevrolet Vega."

GM is underestimating itself. Performance standards will continue to stimulate technological innovations; the Vega is not the last word in combining size and efficiency. And new technologies may not cause unemployment. They may be especially labor intensive. Anyway, the labor content of automobiles varies less with their size than with the optional equipment that adorns them.

The national interest in oil conservation is patent. Domestic production is in the sixth year of decline, a million barrels a day below the level when the embargo began in 1973. We are importing 42 per cent of the oil we use, up from 29 per cent in 1972. One week this spring we set a dismal record: imported oil, and products, exceeded domestic production.

THE BIG-CAR COMEBACK

Automobile efficiency is the heart of the matter. We burn 50 per cent of our oil on highways. In the first eight days of July 1975, vacation travel days, Americans used as much oil as the U.S. Armed Forces used in 1944, the most strenuous year of World War II. But there remains the unassailable core of Reagan's case against the new law: it "regulates the marketplace, dictates to the consumer . . ." Indeed it does.

Everything we know about past and present consumer preferences, and the American psyche, supports Reagan's judgment that unfettered consumer demand would cause Detroit to produce different cars—heavier and more powerful—than Detroit must produce to comply with the law. Big cars are staging a strong comeback. *Vox populi, vox Dei.* Then the voice of God is the voice of the Detroit woman who, when car shopping in May, declared: "I want to buy a car when it's still a car, and not one of those small things."

Volumes of U.S. history are packed into that woman's disdain for "small things." And the essence of Reagan's conservatism is in his defense of her sovereign right to indulge her disdain.

Of course, a government must be generally predisposed to respect the ordinary desires of ordinary people; otherwise it cannot live in harmony with the governed. But Reagan seems more than just generally predisposed. In his enthusiasm for the market mechanism is an unsettling indiscriminateness, a breath of dogmatism and perhaps a confusion about the purpose of government.

There are sober people of understanding and goodwill who believe the new fuel-efficiency standards are mistaken. Reagan's criticism *is* defensible. But the fact that the standards interfere with market choices is not itself a sufficient ground for defense.

At birth (say, for fun, in 1776: the publication of Adam Smith's "Wealth of Nations") the free-market doctrine was utilitarian. It subsequently has become, in some circles, slightly mystical. Some conservatives cling to it with the unreasoning intensity of swimmers clinging to rocks in a riptide.

A free market is a nifty arrangement for recording preferences and allocating resources accordingly. But there is a point at which the obeisance of political persons before market decisions is, like other forms of populism, an excuse for not leading. At that point free-market principles are less an aspect of their political philosophy than a substitute for political philosophy.

A RESPONSIBLE STATE

The state is more than a device for serving the immediate preferences of its citizens. Its purpose is to achieve collective objectives, and the collectivity—the nation—includes a constituency of generations not yet born. That is why the state, unlike an economic market, has *responsibilities*, and must look down the road farther than citizens generally look in their private pursuits. Thus the state's legitimate purposes are more complex than the sum of citizens' private purposes; the public interest is not just the automatic, unguided outcome of the maelstrom of private interests. A conservativism that cannot comfortably accommodate these elementary truths is unserious, and irrelevant to the *political* economy of our nation.

Surely the art, the drama of democratic government derives from this fact: the long-term interests of the nation frequently are not the short-term desires of the majority. Reagan's Detroit remarks, including the tiresome, reflexive denunciation of "elitists," raise doubts about his understanding of that.

Fig. 36. Contemporary potter forming the rim of a vessel in Ban Kham Oo, a village near Ban Chiang.

was also employed throughout prehistoric Southeast Asia. Although there may have been a utilitarian function for impressing cord onto the surface of pottery, it was clearly applied as an aesthetic element in the Ban Chiang ceramics. Cord impressions were applied usually by either of two methods: paddling the pot surface with a cordwrapped paddle (e.g. cat. no. 33), or by rolling a cord-wrapped cylinder down the surface of the pot (e.g., cat. no. 27). Cord width varied considerably from coarse to very fine. Beyond cordmarking, the ancient potter used at one time or another appliqué, rocker stamping, combpricking, freehand painting and incising, and burnishing; often more than one technique was used per pot (e.g., cat. no. 19).

Manufacturing techniques beyond those of the present day were utilized as well by the ancient potter. Additives to the clay included whole rice husks and occasionally sand and laterite. The distinct contours of some pots indicate that methods other than the simple paddle and anvil were used to shape them. In particular the large carinated wares of the Middle Period (cat. nos. 39–44) appear to have been constructed in parts (compound buildings). The sinuous shape of their bases, which among grave assemblages often seemed to have a standard size and shape, suggests that they were paddled over molds, possibly another pot base, before the upper body was added. Although technical analyses have not yet been completed, it is evident from the variation in color, in particular the blackish wares of the Early Period, that some effort at manipulating firing conditions was being made.

The ongoing vitality and creativity of the ceramics made over the course of 4000 years at Ban Chiang make this site stand out in the region. No other site including Non Nok Tha (Bayard 1977) has yet produced ceramics of comparable artistic variety in such quantity. The meaning for this distinctiveness is not yet clear. Ban Chiang appears to be a regional center—but a center for what? It was not located near sources for metal ores or fine-grained stone. It had no monopoly on clay or water resources. The burials showed some social distinctions but suggested overall pros-

Fig. 37. Paddle and anvil technique. The potter forms the body of a pot by beating the exterior with a wooden paddle while she supports the interior with a baked clay anvil. This closes the base and shapes the globular contours of the pot.

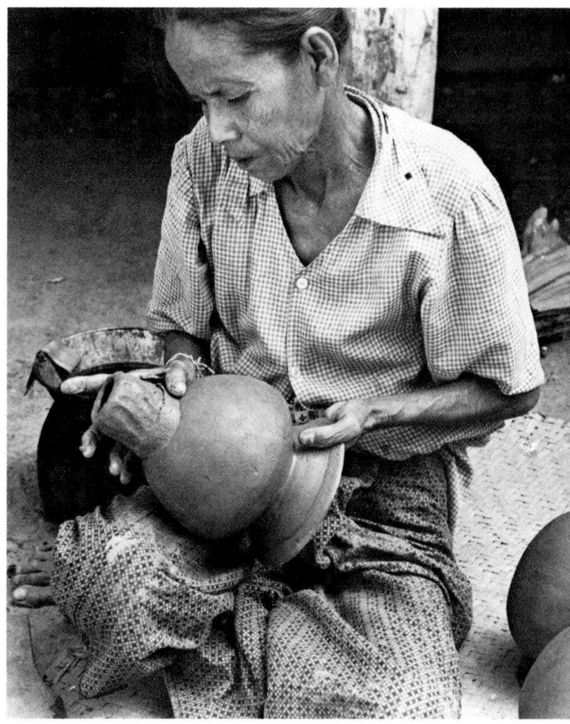

Fig. 38. A foot can be added to the base of the pot.

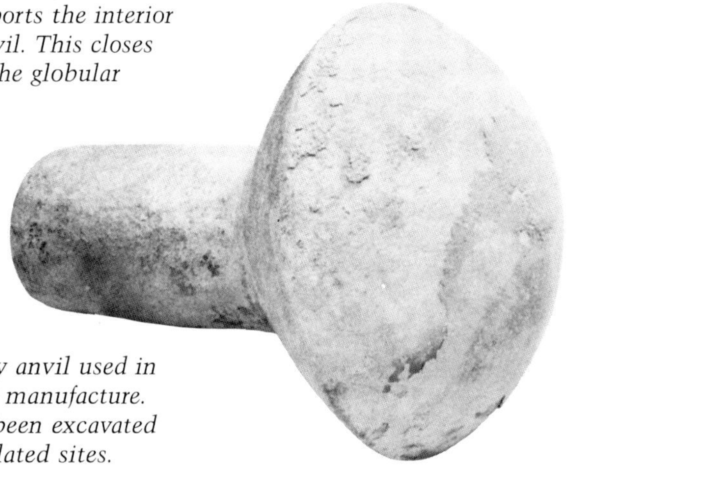

Fig. 39. A baked clay anvil used in contemporary pottery manufacture. Similar objects have been excavated at Ban Chiang and related sites.

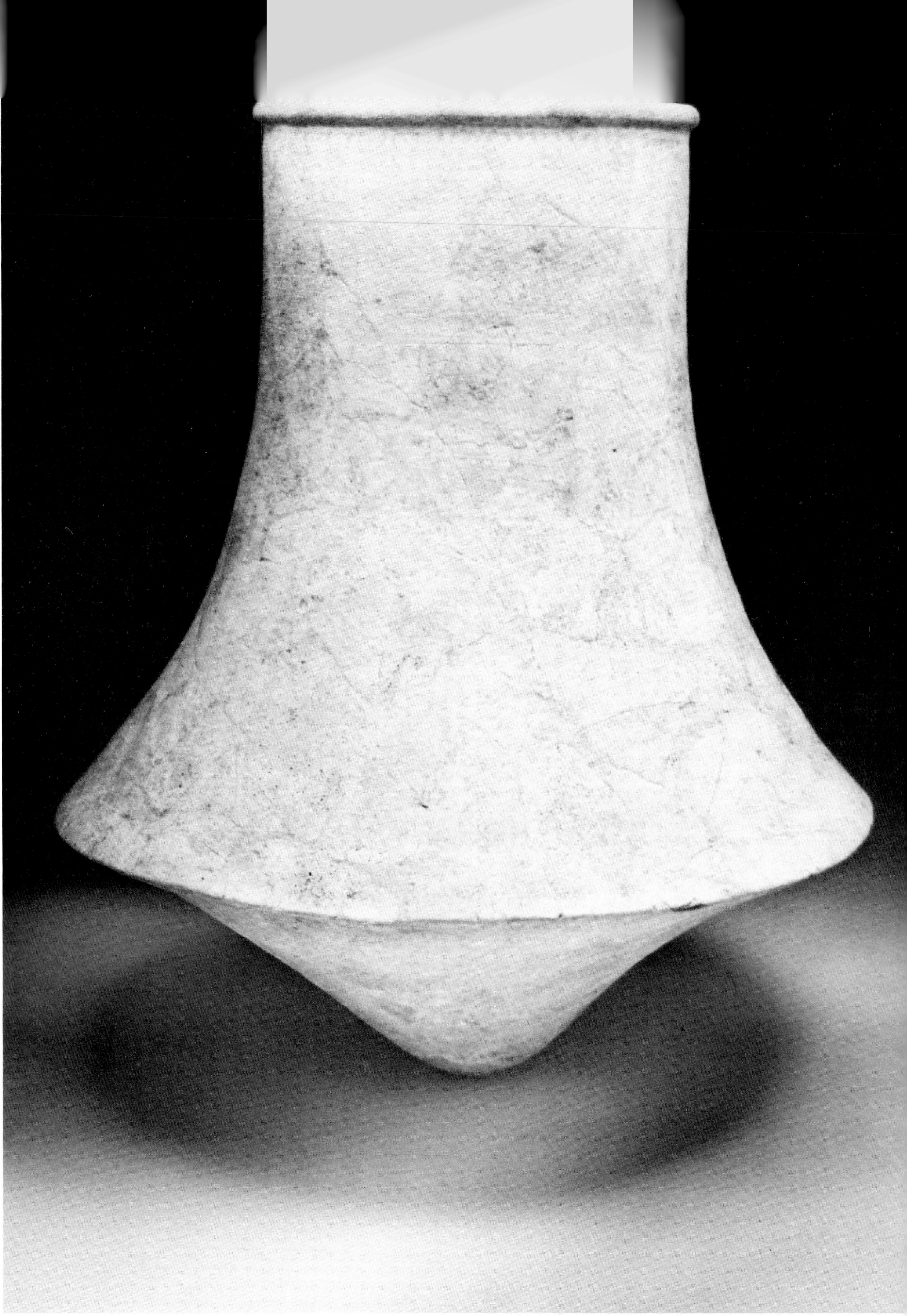

Fig. 40. White carinated pot (cat. no. 39). The bases of these carinated pots may have been formed by paddling clay over molds.

Fig. 41. Cordmarked pot (cat. no. 22). The vertical cordmarking on the upper body of this pot was carefully applied, ostensibly as a decorative element. This pot came from one of the oldest excavated graves at Ban Chiang (BC burial 44).

perity rather than the existence of elite classes. Whatever gave rise to the burgeoning artistic activity remains to be defined through future research.

Ancient Metallurgy of Northeast Thailand

The emergence of metalworking in early villages on the Khorat Plateau signifies that the ancient inhabitants had crossed a threshhold in the understanding and manipulation of their environment. Unlike technologies based on the direct modification of raw materials such as stone, bone, wood, or clay, ductile metals must be extracted from crystalline ores before they can be shaped into useful items. The extraction or smelting of copper is hardly an incidental result of the placement of a copper-bearing ore in an ordinary cooking fire. Not only are higher temperatures required (over 1000 degrees C for smelting copper versus 600 to 800 degrees for an open-cooking fire), but a reducing or oxygen-starved atmosphere is necessary for the chemical reaction to occur. Beyond smelting, a host of other techniques, procedures, plus ancillary equipment need to be developed for productive, efficient utilization of a metal—techniques for mining, alloying, casting, cold working, annealing, and others. Which techniques were known to the early metalsmiths of the Khorat Plateau? How did they use them? How did they acquire the knowledge? Local inspiration? Distant import? And why? What was so valuable or useful about metals to the ancient villagers of northeast Thailand to be worth enduring the heat, the dirt, the exacting tedium, the labor investment necessary to produce metal objects? While our understanding at present of many of these issues is scanty at best, a configuration of the metallurgy of ancient Thailand is beginning to emerge.

The investigation of ancient metallurgy does not turn on the excavation of a single piece of metal, a single date, or even a single site. What is sought is a pattern of knowledge, a pattern of usage, and these patterns emerge from many kinds of clues, often microscopic, from many sites.

Analyses of Metals from Non Nok Tha

One of the most important outgrowths of the Non Nok Tha excavations was the initiation of systematic archaeometallurgical study of Southeast Asian metals. This scientific analysis of ancient metals seeks to reconstruct the knowledge and procedures of the prehistoric metalsmith, and thus to elucidate the history and processes of human technological development. Two major aspects of such study include elemental analysis to help determine the mineral content of an object, and metallographic analysis to help reveal the methods of manufacture.

A primary goal of elemental analysis is to determine whether, if in addition to the base metal, other minerals were deliberately added to form an alloy whose mechanical and physical properties have some advantage over the unalloyed metal. Unalloyed copper, either native (naturally occuring in the metallic state) or smelted, is not notably hard and casts poorly. The addition of tin to copper to form bronze produces a harder, more enduring metal with better casting properties. The proportion of an additive also affects the properties of the alloy, and tin added in the range of 10 to 15 percent optimizes strength while minimizing brittleness. This greatly enhances the utilitarian potential of the metal. An important result of spectro-analytical studies of Non Nok Tha metals (Selimkhanov 1979; Pittioni 1970) is that the preponderance of objects are tin-bronze alloys with the proportion of tin generally in the optimal range. In addition to tin, Pittioni (1970:160) concludes that lead was deliberately added to some artifacts. The addition of lead might have improved casting qualities of the alloy. Such consistent, nearly standardized alloys bespeak a developed level of metallurgical knowledge and skill, well beyond experimental stages or irregular usage.

Fig. 42. Socketed tools from Non Nok Tha, northeast Thailand (top: cat. no. 12, bottom (WOST): cat. no. 11).

Fig. 43. Grave goods from burial 76 (BCES), an Early Period flexed burial: beaker pot (cat. no. 25), socketed bronze spearpoint (cat. no. 92).

Fig. 44. Dendritic structures characteristic of cast bronze. This photomicrograph (x200) is from a specimen of the bronze haft on a bimetallic spearpoint (cat no. 105).

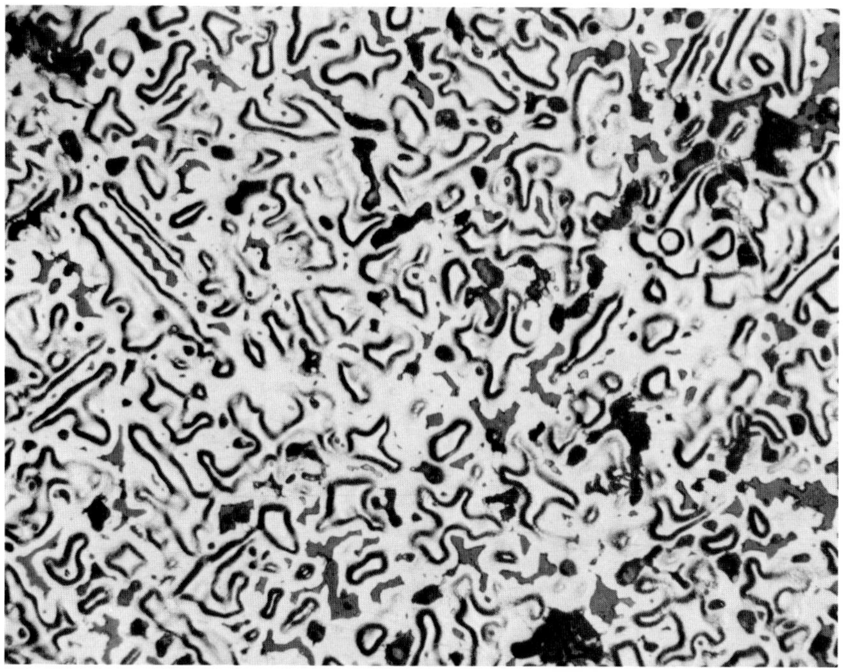

The expertise of the ancient metalsmiths of Non Nok Tha has been further examined by metallographic studies which yielded information on how the objects were fabricated (Smith 1973; Stech Wheeler and Maddin 1976). For this type of study a sample is cut from the object and embedded in a plastic mount with one surface exposed. After the polishing and etching of this surface the grain or microstructures of the metal can be observed with an optical microscope. The image can be recorded with a photomicrograph. Cast bronze items produce branching, fernlike patterns called dendritic structures. Such dendrites were observed in samples from the Non Nok Tha bronze artifacts.

Once an item was cast, the metalsmith might have performed additional procedures that could be detected in the item's microstructures. If an edge were hammered while cold (cold working) in order to strengthen it, the grain structure of the bronze would flatten and dark striae known as strain markings would be visible. Excessive cold working causes the edge to become brittle. This can be alleviated if the object is reheated to a temperature at which the grains of metal recrystallize, a procedure known as annealing. Recrystallization of bronze leaves traces called annealing twins in the microstructure. The object may then again be cold hammered.

Examination of one of the earlier bronze axes from Non Nok Tha (NP 549, fig. 42, cat. no. 12) dated to about 2100 B.C. by the excavators (Bayard, personal communication) demonstrates the impressive technological repertoire of the ancient metalsmith at Non Nok Tha. This artifact showed structural evidence of alloying, casting, cold working, and annealing to shape and strengthen the working edge. The splaying of its cutting edge seems to have been hammered out from a cast of simpler configuration. Smith concludes (1973:28), "Altogether this axe is a result of a fairly advanced metalworking operation fully exploiting the casting and working propensities of bronze." Also studied were bracelets which showed no postcasting treatment; Smith (1973:29) suggests they might have been made by the lost wax process. By-products of metalworking were also analyzed including irregularly shaped bronze nodules showing the undistorted grain structure of cast bronze which were interpreted as drops of molten metal probably spilled during the casting process. This is evidence, along with several bivalve (two piece) sandstone axe molds (cat. nos. 13, 14) and crucibles with dross adhering, that casting was being done at the site.

These metallurgical analyses have revealed considerably more about the level of sophistication of the ancient technology than the mere presence of bronze. However the metals from Non Nok Tha raised many intriguing problems and questions. Where were the sources of ore? How and where was the smelting carried out? Where did the knowledge come from? Was there evidence of a less advanced, more experimental phase of metalworking in the region? Elemental analyses of the earliest metals have yielded contradictory results. One analysis of WOST (fig. 42, cat. no. 11) dated by the excavators to ca. 2700 B.C. (reported in Bayard 1972) indicated that it was an unalloyed copper tool. Ongoing metallographic and elemental analyses should confirm or revise this analysis, but should it turn out to be copper it might be suggestive of a developmental stage, a "Copper Age," preceding the bronze of later periods. On the other hand

Fig. 45. Bronze bangles uncovered in the basal layers of the Thai Fine Arts Department test excavation at Ban Chiang.

Selimkhanov (1979) reports an analysis for metal of equal age at 14 percent tin. Was WOST merely an anomaly?

Bronzes from Ban Chiang

The NETAP excavations at Ban Chiang promised to contribute greatly to the fund of knowledge about the ancient metallurgy of Southeast Asia. Looting activities had produced ample evidence that a wealth of bronze existed at the site (Lyons and Rainey 1982), and Thai Fine Arts Department test excavations had shown that bronze bangles came from low levels (cat. no. 167). But how old was this low bronze? Might there be an experimental phase of copper-based metallurgy at the site? Might the site have been used for smelting ores? As the NETAP excavations sought to unravel some of the questions raised by Non Nok Tha, new unexpected data came to light, and more questions were formulated.

The two seasons of excavation yielded several hundred metal objects the vast majority of which were amorphous corroded fragments. More than one hundred "recognizable" bronze and iron objects were recovered, however, primarily from grave contexts. Several of these have been analyzed and form the basis of this discussion.* The scientist is faced with a bias of unknown dimensions when seeking to generalize about the prehistoric technology on the basis of what the ancients thought appropriate to bury with their dead. Moreover the likelihood that the archaeologist's sample missed important clues must be remembered. Yet grave goods in relatively good condition and with relatively clear provenience are the best place to start. Future research efforts should broaden our understanding.

While not many metal objects from Early Period graves were excavated, those few recovered suggest an advanced stage of metalworking comparable to that of the Non Nok Tha axe (cat. no. 12), employing a similar range of manufacturing skills. One of the lowest metal artifacts recovered from a grave was the socketed spearpoint whose tip had been bent at about a 90 degree angle prior to interment (fig. 43, cat. no. 92). This

*Metals recovered from Ban Chiang and other sites excavated by NETAP have been analysed under the direction of Dr. Robert Maddin and Dr. Tamara Stech (Wheeler). Preliminary findings were reported in *Expedition* (1976). Several students made substantial contributions to the analytical research including Christine Abiera, Surapol Natapintu, Timbul Haryono. Iron artifacts recovered during surveys of the region around Ban Chiang are currently under study by Dr. Vincent Piggott. Dr. Maddin kindly gave his permission to refer to unpublished results of these analyses and Surapol Natapintu greatly assisted in the preparation of this essay. Any errors in interpretation, however, are solely the responsibility of the author.

Fig. 46. Iron artifacts of the Middle Period: clockwise from bottom right, bimetallic spearpoint (fragment) (cat. no. 105), bimetallic bracelet (cat. no. 107), iron bangles (cat. nos. 108, 109), bimetallic spearpoint (cat. no. 106).

Fig. 47. Crucibles (from top, cat. nos. 52, 51, 53).

Fig. 48. Bronze bangles (clockwise from top, cat. nos. 99, 98, 104, 100).

Fig. 49. Flanged bangles of bronze (cat. no. 103) and marble (cat. no. 163).

spearpoint had been placed in the flexed burial of a young man along with a simple beaker type pot (cat. no. 25).

Metallurgical analysis revealed that this artifact may have a very low tin content, 1.3 percent (Stech Wheeler and Maddin 1976), too low to be unequivocably designated as an intentional bronze. However, the method of elemental analysis, optical emission spectrography, has a high margin of error and the tin content may be up to three times higher. It is notable, however, that the lowest metal artifacts at Ban Chiang and Non Nok Tha may have been unalloyed or very low tin-copper alloys. Metallographic analysis showed nevertheless that the spearpoint was still quite a sophisticated object. It was cast in a bivalve mold with a core piece inserted to form the socket, and subsequently was cold hammered and annealed. Thus the same basic technological repertoire evidenced in the Non Nok Tha axehead (cat. no. 12) was found in the earliest metal tool excavated at Ban Chiang.

In another Early Period burial of a five-year-old child several bronze anklets were recovered (cat. no. 93). Metallographic analyses showed that these were cast bronze with no postcasting treatment. Thus during the Early Period it appears that the ornamental use of metals coexisted with the utilitarian use, a pattern which extends throughout the metal sequence.

One burial from the latter part of the Early Period (ca. 1600–1300 B.C.) contained both utilitarian and ornamental bronzes. The prominence of the bronze grave goods led this burial to be dubbed "Vulcan" by fieldworkers. On the left wrist of this middle-aged male were four bracelets with a simple circular cross section (cat. no. 95). At his left shoulder was placed a well-made bronze socketed "axe" or, given its placement in the grave with one lateral point downward and the socket facing away from the body more likely an adze (fig. 50, cat. no. 94). Even though the object appears to be utilitarian, it is possible that it was not used before being buried. Analysis of the edge showed no evidence for cold hammering or annealing to harden it.

During the Middle Period (ca. 1000–300 B.C.) and Late Period (ca. 300 B.C.–A.D. 200) no bronze utilitarian artifacts were recovered from graves, but bronze ornaments, mostly anklets and bracelets, were common. The shapes show considerable elaboration over the plain rings of the Early Period (fig. 48). A magnificent flanged, "T"-section bracelet was worn by a middle-aged man buried under a sheet of sherds from nine carinated pots (burial 40, BCES). He wore an identical style bracelet in calcite as well. This flanged style in various materials (fig. 49, cat. no. 163) is widespread in prehistoric contexts throughout Southeast Asia. Other bangle shapes include spirals and "C" rings; cross sections may be square, "D"-shaped, or flat. Sometimes special details have come to light only after conservation of the piece. Three bangles separated by the conservator from one seemingly solid ring turned out to be a set clearly made to be worn together (fig. 48, cat. no. 104). The two outer rings had contoured scallops on the outer surfaces, their inner surfaces were flat. The central ring was flat on both sides, but was notched to match the profile of the scallops of the external rings. Such attention to sets of items seems particularly characteristic of the Middle Period when sets of similar pots were shattered over the graves. Metallographic analyses show the bangles of the Middle Period to be cast bronzes with no postcasting treatment.

No evidence for the smelting of ores was recovered from Ban Chiang. Since little or no slag—the solidified residue which is a by-product of smelting ores—has been recovered from the sites excavated thus far in

Fig. 50. Early Period burial with adze and bracelets (Vulcan, BC burial 23).

northeast Thailand, archaeologists think that smelting may have taken place near ore sources scattered around the rim of the Khorat Plateau. One possible mining area might have been in what is today Loei province where a small mountain called Copper Mountain (Phu Thong Daeng) has large deposits of low grade (1 percent) copper ore (Workman 1972:37).

Eventually, elemental analyses of both bronze artifacts and slag will help reconstruct smelting processes and may help trace ore sources. Different ores produce copper of varying qualities and, moreover, require distinctive smelting strategies. Since several of the Ban Chiang artifacts contain copper sulfide or copper iron sulfide (Dr. Robert Maddin, personal communication), this suggests that the ore may have been a partially weathered chalocopyrite. Because such sulfide ores do not smelt efficiently, they require that their sulfur content be reduced prior to smelting. Though it is by no means clear, it is commonly held that the ores were roasted in open fires to drive off the sulfur. If the use of these difficult sulfide ores can be corroborated, it further supports the emerging picture of the proficiency of the ancient Southeast Asian metalsmith.

During the second season at Ban Chiang, excavators found an area with masses of baked clay and scattered remains of crucibles, some virtually intact (fig. 47, cat. nos. 51–53). This cultural feature was interpreted as a casting area and was found just above the interface of the lower greyish soil with the upper reddish stratum, that is, at the early part of the Middle Period. Reconstruction of casting procedures, given current archaeological knowledge, is quite hypothetical, but knowledge of basic requirements and some modern-day practices can help us visualize what might have taken place. Since we have no substantive evidence, such as large piles of slag, that metals were smelted at Ban Chiang or Non Nok Tha or other sites already excavated, we can hypothesize that smelted metals were brought to the site perhaps in ingot form for remelting and casting.

The clay crucibles give some clues as to the casting process. The clay fabric is heavily tempered with whole rice husks, clearly visible on examination with the naked eye. The silica in the husks may have helped prevent the crucible from breaking from thermal shock resulting from the temperatures necessary to melt the ingots (copper melts at 1083 degress C). Both the Non Nok Tha and Ban Chiang crucibles show no effects of fire on their external surfaces (Smith 1973:30), hence Smith suggests that the fuel would have been placed on top of the crucible in direct contact with the metal pieces of copper ingot.

Inside many of the crucibles are greyish-greenish concretions which may be dross. These impurities separate from and float on the molten metal and cling to the crucible when the metal is poured off. Many crucibles have a red stain on the interior which could come from a number of sources. It may derive either from iron naturally occuring in the copper ores, or from the iron oxide hematite, which might have been added during the smelting process as a flux—an additive to facilitate the separation of impurities.

Melting the metals requires high constant temperatures and hence a concerted effort. The masses of baked clay in association with the crucibles suggest that heating took place in clay-lined pits into which the crucible filled with metal and fuel could be placed. Raising the temperature to over 1000 degrees C would require a constant direct stream of air on the coals. The ancient metalsmith might have simply blown through a hollow bamboo tube. At some point, however, an important technological innovation, the double piston type of bellows found all over Southeast Asia, may have been developed. Piston bellows can be made from large

Fig. 51. Vulcan's grave goods: clockwise from top, baked clay pellets (cat. no. 36), bronze adze (cat. no. 94), painted and incised pot (fragment) (cat. no. 35), bronze bracelets (cat. no. 95).

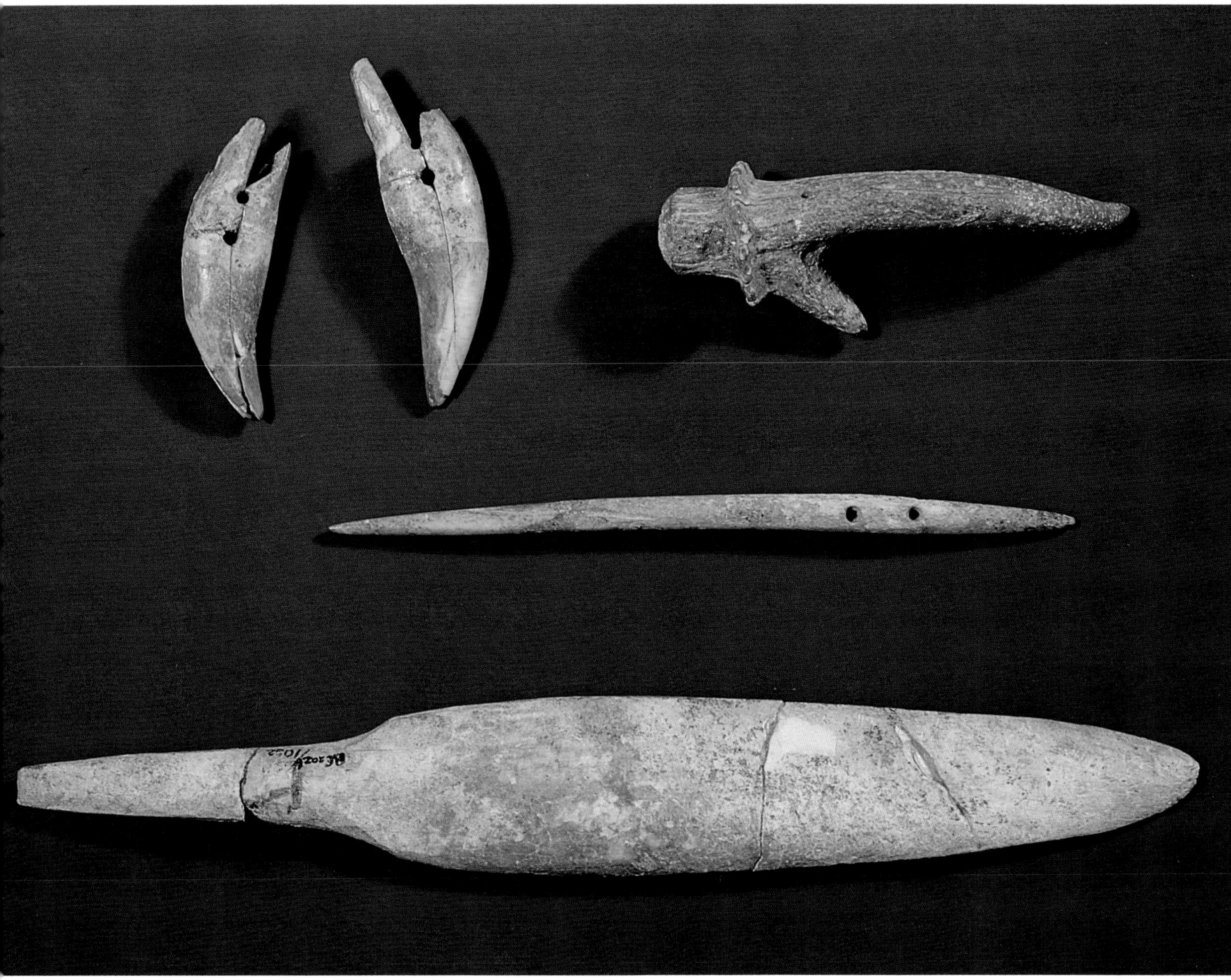

Fig. 52. Nimrod's worked bone grave assemblage: from top left, drilled tiger's teeth (cat. no. 129), carved antler (cat. no. 128), drilled "hairpin" (cat. no. 126), spearpoint (cat. no. 127).

bamboo tubes or hollowed out wooden logs which then are fitted with plungers. Such bellows are still widely used by blacksmiths in northeast Thailand today, although they are rapidly being replaced by corrogated tin bellows and even electric blowers. A pair of piston bellows is operated by one individual who alternately pumps the plungers. Tubes called tuyeres extend from the base of the bellows and direct the stream of air directly onto the coals. These are sometimes tipped with clay to prevent burning.

Once the metal is molten the crucible needs to be quickly removed from the hearth, perhaps by two individuals clasping it between green sticks, and the metal poured into waiting molds. Utilitarian items such as the socketed spearpoint and adze were cast in symmetrical bivalve molds with a core piece inserted to form the socket. Such a casting technique is much more elaborate than that used to produce the flat cast, tanged tools that characterize early cast implements in many other parts of the Old World. The bangles and bells may have been made in lost wax molds.

Unlike Non Nok Tha where several pairs of bivalve sandstone axe molds were recovered, only a few mold fragments were encountered in the NETAP excavations at Ban Chiang. This difference might have been due to a functional distinction between the two sites. Non Nok Tha, which is located near to potential ore sources in the Petchabun Mountains, might have specialized in producing axes. Also the sources for sandstone to make the molds can be found in a nearby mountain. Ban Chiang is not located near sources of either sandstone or ores and might have received most implements ready-made. On the other hand Ban Chiang people could have made clay molds and used the lost wax process for casting, the remnants of which might be harder to recover or identify in the archaeological record. Sample bias, the chance that the excavation locales produced this distinction between the two sites, is another possible explanation. The elucidation of the regional network for producing and exchanging metals and metal products will be one of the prime areas of future research in northeast Thailand.

Iron at Ban Chiang

The most important and unanticipated discovery of the Middle Period (ca. 1000–300 B.C.) was the presence of iron artifacts, some of the oldest iron objects in East Asia (fig. 46). The artifacts include iron bangles found on the burial of a five-year-old child (cat. nos. 108–110), a bimetallic bracelet (cat. no. 107) with a bronze bangle encircled by iron rings which had either been wrapped around the inner bangle or had slipped over it and corroded over time into place, and two bimetallic (bronze and iron) spearpoints (cat. nos. 105, 106). A radiograph showed that bronze hafts had been cast on to nubs extending from the forged iron blade.

The appearance of iron in the Middle Period indicates considerable expansion in the metallurgical repertoire of the ancient metalsmith. The melting point of iron, about 1530 degrees C, is a very high temperature difficult to achieve in the simpler forms of furnaces. Iron will smelt at about the same temperature as copper given proper conditions. However it is more difficult to smelt with the same direct smelting method used with copper ores since it requires considerable amounts of charcoal to produce carbon monoxide sufficient to create the reducing atmosphere necessary in the smelting furnace.

The main technique for early iron smelting in antiquity usually has been the bloomery process. In this process, metallic iron is reduced from the ore in the solid state. The resulting product of the bloomery process was a spongy mass of iron and slag called a "bloom," which was still not pure enough for forging a tool. The entrapped slag was removed by reheating the bloom until it was almost white-hot (this required a temperature greater than 1000 degrees C), followed by forging. The remaining slag thus was squeezed out of the bloom by means of hammering. Repeated heating and hammering squeezed out most of the slag and consolidated the bloom. The resultant product then was a "wrought iron," which is pure iron with a minimum slag content that was shaped into desired objects.

Shaping objects out of wrought iron differs from casting copper or bronze items in that a significant number of man hours together with physical effort must go into the forging process. Forging objects by hammering the hot iron into the desired shape was usually the preferred technique for ancient iron working, except in China where a strong tradition of cast iron evolved. Forging required that a new range of implements for working iron be developed, such as tongs, hammers, anvils. However, since wrought iron is not a very hard metal, it only became a truly useful metal when the process of intentional steeling was developed. In this process the forged wrought iron object is reheated to temperatures in excess of 900 degrees C for a considerable period. During the heating carbon from the charcoal will continuously, but very slowly, diffuse atom-by-atom into the heated iron. However, the steeling process is time- and fuel-consuming, which during primitive forging may not be efficiently applied. Thus while an iron tool may be heated for several hours, carbon may diffuse into it only part of a millimeter (Maddin et al. 1977). Therefore, only a thin outer layer of the iron tool may be steeled (case-hardened), its core remaining a wrought iron. After a prolonged period of heating, the hot steeled iron may be suddenly quenched by plunging it into cold water. The carbon, which has diffused into the iron during the heating cycle will be trapped in the crystal structure of the iron, thus hardening the iron.

So little is presently known about the iron technology at Ban Chiang that it is difficult to make general statements. We have no remains of iron working implements, no evidence for the sources of ore utilized or smelting procedures undertaken. A few clues suggest that the iron artifacts were not unique odd objects or foreign imports, but rather were of local manufacture. Analysis of the bimetallic spearpoints provided not only evidence for slight carburization (not enough to indicate a steel), but also evidence sufficient to indicate the production of wrought, not cast iron. This contrasts with the Chinese iron technology which produced predominantly cast iron implements. Only trace amounts of nickel were detected in the Ban Chiang iron (Stech Wheeler and Maddin 1976)

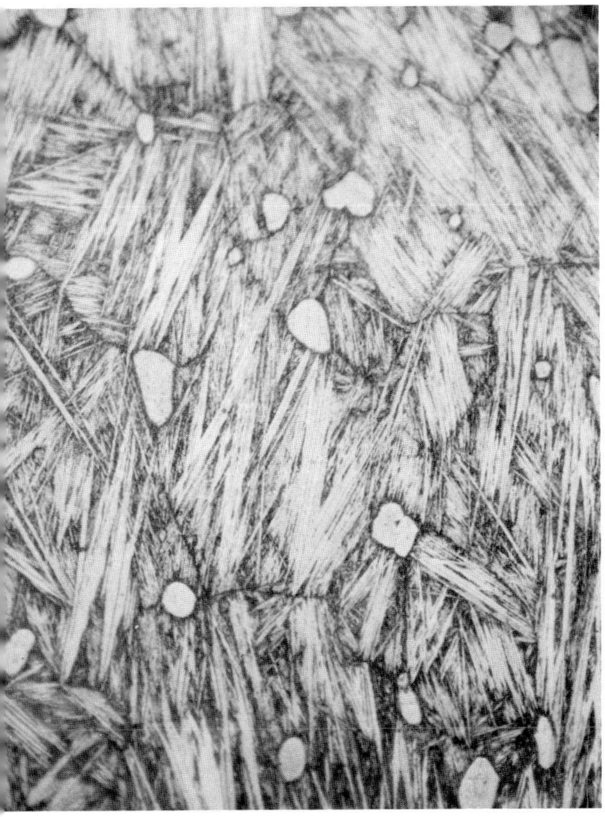

Fig. 53. Optical micrograph (x500) showing needlelike microstructures characteristic of high tin bronze which has undergone a solid state martensitic transformation. Specimen was from a wire fragment excavated at Don Klang, a site near Non Nok Tha (DK 209/381).

implying that the iron was smelted from an ore. Again this contrasts with analyses of the earliest iron objects from China whose high nickel content indicates that they were fashioned directly from meteoritic iron which requires no smelting. Thus the technology of the Ban Chiang iron appears distinctive from its nearest neighbor.

Most importantly we find the continuation of the cultural pattern of contemporaneous use of a metal for both ornamental bangles and utilitarian implements, just as with the Early Period bronzes. But as in the bronze technology we have no evidence for experimental stages. The bimetallic spearpoints with midribs are well thought out and elegantly made, not clumsy experiments. Aesthetics may have played a role in the combination of the two metals: the yellowish bronze socket and blackish iron blade combined to make a handsome implement. We must again appeal to future research to clarify how iron technology was acquired by the ancient villagers of Ban Chiang.

Late Period Metals

During the Late Period no iron ornaments were found, but iron continued to be used for tools and weapons. Bronze continued in use as an ornamental medium in bangles and bells especially, but a new and highly sophisticated variant appeared. The analysis of rods from a multistrand necklace of a five- or six-year-old child, referred to as "Bianca" by the excavators, produced startling results. The needlelike structures evident in the photomicrographs revealed that a bronze of unusually high tin content had undergone a martensitic transformation. Such a transformation occurs when a bronze of more than 20 percent tin is specially handled. Such a high tin bronze is too hard and too brittle to be cold-worked into the thin necklace strands. The martensitic transformation indicates that the wires were made while hot—between 550 to 750 degrees C. At these temperatures the bronze is plastic and the thin rods might have been cut from sheets of metal. Frequent reheating would have been necessary to cut the several strips. If the metal were allowed to cool slowly as in the annealing process, the metal would have remained extremely brittle. However, these wires were suddenly dropped into water (quenched) so they remained hard but much less brittle. It is this quenching action that causes the martensitic, or solid state transformation of the bronze to occur. Stech Wheeler and Maddin suggest that the original hue of this bronze would have been silverish, hence the metalsmith might have been aiming to imitate silver for aesthetic reasons. This particular technology is considered to be quite sophisticated by metallurgists. That it was used to make delicate necklaces for children at Ban Chiang is astounding and unprecedented in prehistory. Subsequent analyses of wires from other sites in northeast Thailand (e.g., cat. no. 115) indicate this technology was widely used in the region.

The Peaceful Bronze Age

Our ideas of what the Bronze Age signifies have been shaped in large part by more than one hundred years' excavation in the Near East and the Mediterranean Basin. Decades of research there have revealed the processes of metallurgical development from a few hammered trinkets in early villages, to inlaid bronze vessels in royal repositories. Production of true tin-bronzes flourished during the third millennium B.C. with the rise of the Mesopotamian urban civilization. Intimate interdependence of bronze and the city-state is evident in the weaponry and ceremonial items found in the centers. Beyond the technical knowledge, complex societies seemed to provide the proper social context for the regular organized production of metal artifacts. In particular the mining and smelting stages appeared to require organized cooperative effort to provide large quantities of both ore and fuel needed to extract a proportionately small quantity of metal. Later there is some specific evidence for the use of forced labor especially for the labor-intensive mining and smelting operations. Moreover, long distance trade networks arose to meet the demand for tin, a scarce mineral in the ancient Near East and Mediterranean regions.

Given the detailed evidence for the development of metallurgy in the Near East, including thousands of years of experimenting with ores and alloys plus the technically complex series of processes involved before the right recipes for durable, efficiently produced items were developed, it has for some time been assumed that metallurgy must have had a single source in the Near East from which the technology spread by migration and diffusion to the rest of the Old World.

Scholars working in the Far East have challenged the single center theory. As the northern Chinese Bronze Age became better known and dated, its extraordinary multipiece mold casting of ritual vessels and advanced knowledge of kilns dating from Neolithic times suggested little relationship with the Bronze Age tradition of the West—except for the

Fig. 54. Carved clay rollers of the Late Period (left to right, top, cat. nos. 62, 57, 71, 65; bottom, cat. nos. 59, 69, 60, 58).

Fig. 55. Plowing rice paddies in northeast Thailand. (Photo by William Schauffler.)

fact that bronze per se seemed to have appeared in the Near East before it appeared in China. If the concept of metallurgy perhaps through trade or itinerant smiths did somehow travel the 2500 miles between these two regions, then the uses to which it was put and the technology of manufacture derived from uniquely Chinese inspiration. One of the arguments supporting an exogenous origin for the basic concepts of metallurgy in China is that no satisfactory experimental stage or developmental sequence comparable to that found in the Near East that could have led to the Chinese Bronze Age has ever been delineated. With the exception of a few "awls," knives, and ornaments from preceding cultural phases, the sophisticated alloying and piece-mold casting technology so characteristic of Chinese bronzes seems to have suddenly sprung up during the early Shang dynasty.

The Southeast Asian Metallurgical Province

The discovery of a distinctive metallurgical tradition in Southeast Asia of an antiquity at least comparable to that of northern China, if not earlier, has added new pieces to the puzzle of metallurgical origins. Although the evidence for this tradition has just begun to be unearthed and analyzed, even the earliest excavated metal artifacts reveal a fully competent knowledge of the basic chemical and mechanical properties of bronze. In addition, the early appearance of iron and the early and unique utilization of the high tin-bronze imply an ongoing vitality and innovation in the metal technology of the region.

That this technological precocity occurred in simple village contexts that derived their subsistence from hunting and gathering and simple cultivation is most intriguing. No urban, state, or military stimulus from within or outside the region is in evidence. No complex, stratified social organization appears to have been a cause or a consequence of the development of metal technology.

The types of metal artifacts manufactured by the people of the Ban Chiang tradition and elsewhere in Southeast Asia reflect this nonurban, nonmilitary context. Rather than maceheads or ritual vessels, metal artifacts from both excavated and unprovenienced contexts are either personal ornaments, such as bangles or bells, or utilitarian items, such as axes, arrowheads, and fishhooks. While the spearpoints might have been used for aggressive purposes, they do not seem to have been manufactured on the scale or with the elaboration found in the weaponry of the state civilizations. The Ban Chiang spearpoints might just as likely have been made for hunting, which we know was a vital activity for their subsistence. The distribution of metal artifacts in the graves does not suggest that metal was a major symbol of wealth monopolized by an elite group. Bronze and iron bangles most frequently adorned the arms and legs of children. In sum, we find a metallurgical tradition flourishing in peaceful agrarian village societies, with the metal put to uses appropriate to those societies.

Many questions immediately arise, most of which cannot be answered because vast tracts of not only northeast Thailand, but Southeast Asia, southern China, and western China remain archaeologically a *terra incognita.*

Fig. 56. Sandstone axe mold excavated from Non Nok Tha with modern cast (cat no. 14).

Fig. 57. (Overleaf). Excavating at Ban Chiang.

Where did the Ban Chiang Cultural Tradition originate? Evidence for a cultural transition between Hoabinhian hunter-gatherers in the Spirit Cave area of northern Thailand and the lowland agriculturalists of the Ban Chiang tradition has been sought in the Petchabun Mountains situated between the two areas (Penny 1982; Bayard 1980). These surveys failed to find any evidence for such a transition. However reports on recent archaeological activity in northern Vietnam (Davidson 1975, 1979) indicate that such transitional phases between upland and lowland oriented societies may be in evidence there—which as the crow flies is only about 300 kilometers from northeast Thailand. The possibility of a connection between the settlers of the Khorat Plateau and prehistoric developments in Vietnam and the other countries of the region should be a primary focus for future research.

How did the metallurgical technology arise in the region? No experimental prebronze stages of metallurgy have yet been delineated for the region, but then no cultural connection with external sources has been demonstrated either.

Did the metallurgical tradition of Southeast Asia influence metallurgy in other regions? Again, no direct connections have been demonstrated. However one linguist argues that the Chinese language borrowed the words for copper, iron, tin/lead from Austro-Thai, a Southeast Asian language family (Benedict 1975:316). If the words were borrowed, perhaps the technology was borrowed too.

Why did the exacting, labor-consuming technology of bronze working become established at such an early date in Southeast Asian village contexts? Since this finding does not fit traditional theories, new models will need to be developed. An examination of natural resources available in the region is one possible avenue for research. Sources of fine-grained stone suitable for adzes necessary to clear forests and build houses are notably scarce in the region, while on the other hand copper and tin are both regionally available (Workman 1972). This may help to explain the prominence of adzes in the inventory of early bronze artifacts in the region.

But to focus exclusively on the metal is to miss much of the story and significance of Ban Chiang. Metals do not create cultural development, people do. Whatever the source or influence of the ancient metallurgy of Southeast Asia, it can no longer be denied that social and economic developments in the region from prehistory onward had profound impact in far-flung regions of the world. The impact can be seen in the spread of languages derived from mainland Southeast Asia all over the Indo-Pacific, even to Madagascar (Goodenough, this publication). It is reflected in the dispersal of rice agriculture to Japan and beyond, and the cultivation of many other Southeast Asian derived species in dispersed islands of the Pacific.

The significance of the excavations at Ban Chiang is that they have afforded a view of some 4000 years of the vitality and cultural dynamics of the region that spawned these phenomena. That so many questions remain to be answered means that this region will be one of the most exciting areas for archaeological research for years to come.

BAN CHIANG
In World Ethnological Perspective

by
Ward H. Goodenough

Ban Chiang does more for students of human history than provide evidence of early civilization in Thailand. It gives a new perspective to a long-standing ethnological question involving Southeast Asia, Indonesia, and the Pacific Islands, and it suggests the direction in which we should look for our answer. This question, so perplexing to anthropologists, has been to explain the truly amazing distribution of the hundreds of languages in the Austronesian (or Malayo-Polynesian) language family. The languages in this family—like those in the Indo-European family, to which English belongs—all show the systematic correspondences of vocabulary that demonstrate their descent from a common ancestral language (long extinct) that was spoken an estimated six thousand or more years ago. The Austronesian language family, moreover, appears to be linked with the Thai-Kadai family of languages (which includes Thai, Lao, and some language pockets in Vietnam and southeastern China) in a superfamily, called Austro-Thai (Benedict 1975). This superfamily will be discussed later.

As for the Austronesian languages themselves, what is amazing about their distribution is the geographic extent. Austronesian languages are found from Madagascar in the western extreme, throughout Malaysia, Indonesia, and the Philippines, in enclaves in Vietnam and Taiwan, in pockets along the north coast of New Guinea, and through all the islands of the Pacific Ocean out to and including Hawaii, the Marquesas Islands, and Easter Island at the eastern extreme. This distribution extends more than halfway around the world. It represents movements of people over long distances at sea that took place in prehistory extending back considerably in time. There has been nothing comparable to it in the record of human history other than the spread around the world from western Europe of Indo-European languages (English, Dutch, Spanish, and Portuguese) within the past five hundred years. But how and why did this happen? What was the occasion or the succession of occasions that stimulated this vast movement of people? And where did it begin?

The Southeast Asian mainland and the arc of off-lying islands from Taiwan through the Philippines to Indonesia have appeared for several reasons to comprise the general region within which the Austronesian homeland lies. It is a region closer to centers of early civilization and population growth. Within it are representatives of all the anciently differentiated branches of the Austronesian language family, only some of which are found outside the area. Botanical evidence indicates that it is the area where we find the nearest wild relatives of the domesticated plants in use by Austronesian-speaking peoples everywhere—such crops as yams, taro, arrowroot, and sugarcane, and such tree crops as coconuts, bananas, and breadfruit. Furthermore, there is a greater homogeneity of physical type among Austronesian-speaking peoples in insular Southeast Asia, while there is greater heterogeneity, suggesting the assimilation of other peoples, outside that region, as in Madagascar, in eastern Indonesia, and in the islands of the Pacific Ocean.

In consideration of the botanical evidence relating to the crops associated with Austronesian-speaking peoples, the geographer Carl Sauer suggested in 1936 that Southeast Asia must have been a center of early crop domestication, comparable to but independent of the ancient Near East, and in consequence of such domestication another ancient center of

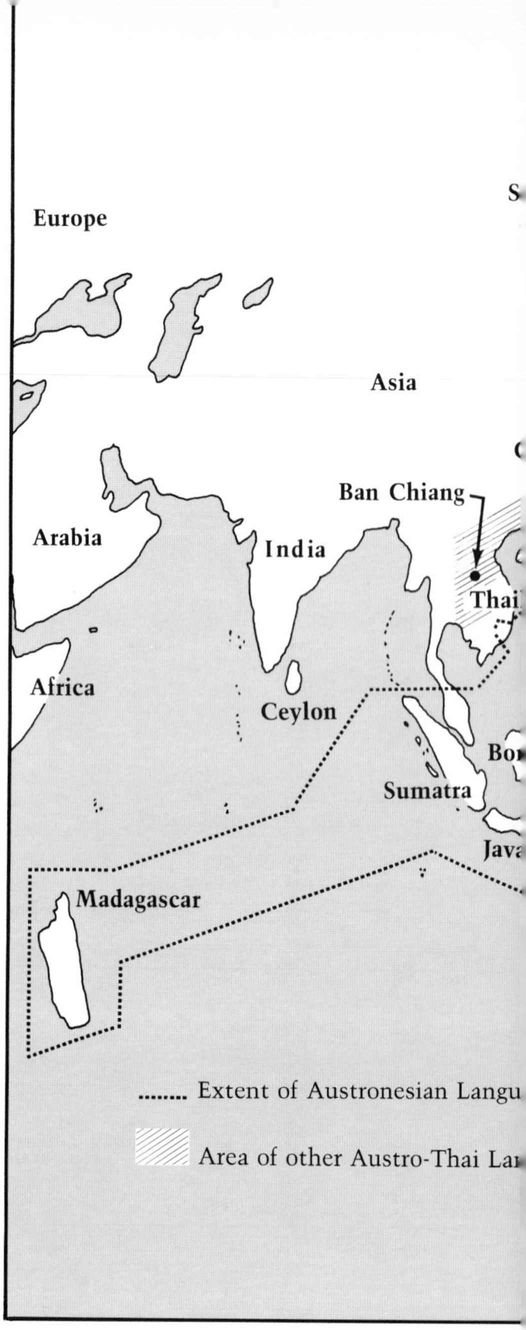

developing civilization and population growth. But prior to the recent work at Ban Chiang and at other archaeological sites in Thailand, there was no archaeological evidence to support this inference, and Sauer's suggestion remained just that, an unverified suggestion.

In the meantime, the findings both of comparative linguistic research and of archaeological excavation in the Pacific Islands kept adding to the puzzle. A strong case was developed that the Austronesian family of languages is itself part of the larger superfamily called Austro-Thai, referred to previously. Comparative study seems to indicate that this ancestral Austro-Thai language contained words for domesticated plants and animals and that these words were borrowed as loan words into the ancient Chinese language (Benedict 1975), much as English contains words borrowed from Latin and Old French. Work on the Austronesian languages also suggests that speakers of the parent language from which

Ward Goodenough is a professor and former chairman of the Department of Anthropology, University of Pennsylvania. He specializes in the languages and cultures of Oceania.

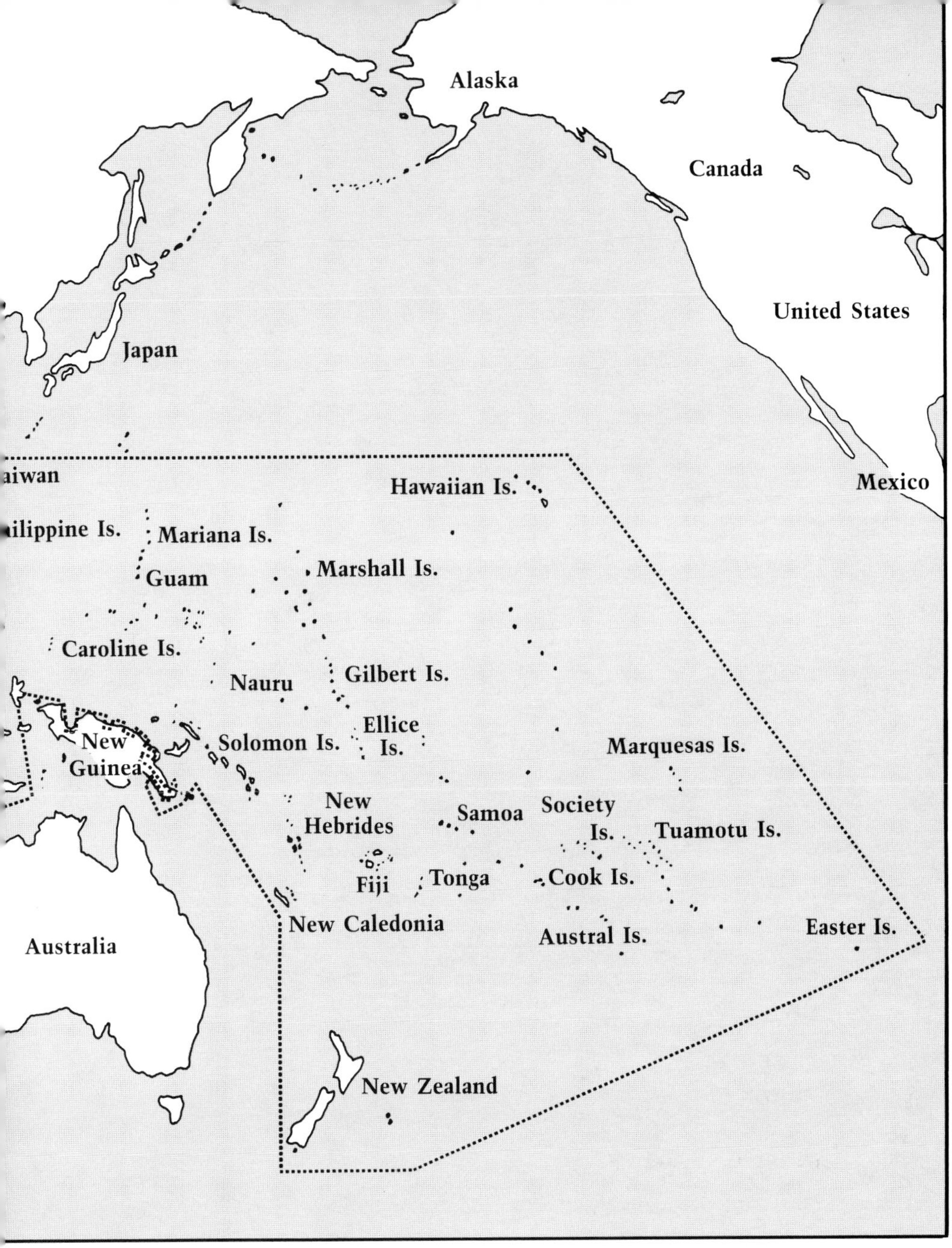

they are descended, as linguists have been able to reconstruct it through comparative study, used words relating to rice cultivation and metal tools (Blust 1976). Clearly the spread of Austronesian speakers was from an ancestral homeland where horticulture, domesticated animals, and metallurgy were known. The distribution of the languages in the coordinate Thai-Kadai family from Thailand northeastward into Vietnam and southern China suggests that this Austronesian homeland was in mainland Southeast Asia. But how far back in time was it before out-migration from that homeland began? On purely linguistic grounds we estimate that differentiation among Austronesian languages must have begun by at least 4000 B.C., but such differentiation could have been taking place on the mainland of Asia for some time prior to any overseas migration. Here is where archaeology helps.

Archaeological research in the Pacific is now showing that settlement there, presumably by speakers of Austronesian languages, goes back a surprisingly long way (Bellwood 1979). By as early as 1500 B.C., for example, the makers of Lapita pottery—a pottery we can associate with the first Polynesian settlements of Tonga and Samoa—were already settled in Fiji in the central Pacific. Before 1000 B.C., makers of this same pottery were also settled in New Caledonia, the New Hebrides, and the Bismarck Archipelago; and makers of a different style of pottery were settled by this time in Saipan in the Mariana Islands. Such early dates are consistent with the degree of linguistic differentiation among speakers of Austronesian languages in the Pacific today. (Archaeological evidence of horticulture in the big island of New Guinea goes back much farther in time, but given the amount of time involved and the absence of Austronesian languages in the interior of New Guinea, it is unlikely that this development of horticulture was associated with the spread of Austronesian-speaking peoples.)

It is reasonable to assume that economic or commerical interests of some kind were responsible for the enormous spread of Austronesian-speaking peoples. These interests, we must presume, were fostered by some developing center of wealth and population on the Asian mainland that provided a growing demand for products from abroad. China, for example, has long been a major importer from Borneo of such forest products as birds' nests, rattan, resins, incense wood, camphor, beeswax, gutta-percha latex, besoar stones, rhinoceros horns, and hornbill ivory and feathers (Hoffman 1982). A trade based on this kind of product demand in the South China Sea in the third and second millenia B.C. to feed into an expanding mainland market would have provided the impetus needed for overseas exploration and settlement. With this expansion there would also have developed secondary centers of population and wealth in Indonesia and the Philippines that would have stimulated further commercial exploration. The spread of Austronesian-speaking peoples makes sense as an outgrowth of this kind of process.

The great problem has been that until the excavation of Ban Chiang, we have had no evidence of any developing center of wealth and population on the Southeast Asian and South Chinese mainland at a sufficiently early date. The famous site of Dong So'n in northern Vietnam appears to have been much too late. Ban Chiang gives us the first direct archaeological evidence of such a center. Ban Chiang itself was probably a fairly peripheral site in relation to the larger region of developing wealth. There should be many more sites like Ban Chiang in northern Vietnam and in southeastern China. Indeed, a survey made by Chester Gorman in northern Vietnam shortly before he died revealed evidence to this effect.

Ban Chiang, then, provides direct evidence of social and cultural developments in Southeast Asia that promises to provide a reasonable explanation for the enormous early dispersal of Austronesian peoples. Ban Chiang transforms our view of the prehistory of the Indonesian and Pacific islands every bit as much as it does our understanding of the prehistory of the East Asian mainland. It all goes together.

Catalogue of the Exhibition

The exhibition consists primarily of artifacts excavated by the Northeast Thailand Archaeological Project (NETAP) at Ban Chiang and related sites. These are on loan from the Fine Arts Department of Thailand. Supplementary items are lent by the National Museum of Thailand and The University Museum, University of Pennsylvania. In general, catalogue entries are grouped by provenience. Items from Tham Pha Chan, Non Nok Tha, and Ban Chiang and related sites excavated by the NETAP are followed by unprovenienced materials and ethnographic items. Within each grouping entries are arranged by medium and chronology. After a brief designation of each item an approximate date is given when known, and artifacts excavated from Ban Chiang are placed in Early (ca. 3600–1000 B.C.), Middle (ca. 1000–300 B.C.), or Late (ca. 300 B.C.–A.D. 200) periods.

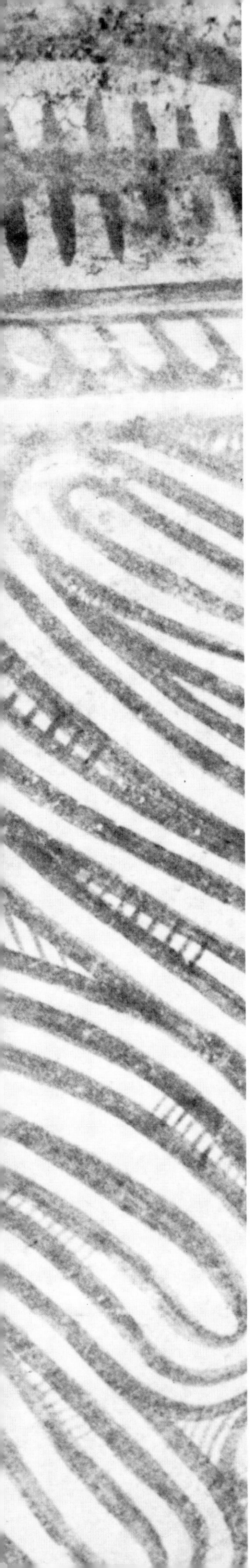

Dimensions in centimeters are taken directly from the ojects. The final line of each entry consists of site reference numbers and museum accession numbers as appropriate. These reference numbers may include the following designations as applicable:

Burial number: At each season of excavation at each site, burials were assigned sequential numbers as they were excavated.

Pot letter: At Ban Chiang each pot from a burial or other cultural feature usually received a letter designation.

Excavation season abbreviations:

NP—the 1966 excavation at Non Nok Tha referred to at that time as Nam Phong 7.

NNT—the 1968 excavation at Non Nok Tha.

BC—the 1974 excavation at Ban Chiang (NETAP).

BCES—the 1975 excavation at Ban Chiang in the eastern soi, or "road" (NETAP).

DK—the 1975 test excavation at Don Klang (NETAP).

BT—the 1975 test excavation at Ban Tong. (NETAP).

BPT—the 1975 test excavation at Ban Phak Top (NETAP).

Small find number: Small find (SF) numbers were assigned at NETAP sites to all discrete artifacts such as bracelets, rollers, pellets, etc., but excluding sherds, pots, charcoal, unworked animal bone and human bone which received bag numbers. Small find numbers are usually followed by a slash and a bag number.

Bag number: These numbers generally follow excavation initials unless preceded by a small find number and a slash(/).

Museum accession numbers: Accession numbers follow objects which have been accessioned by the National Museum of Thailand or The University Museum.

Cat. no. 151 (detail).

2

Hoabinhian Stone Tools of Tham Pha Chan, Northern Thailand

10

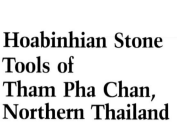

Although the immediate precursors to the lowland settlers at Ban Chiang have not yet been found, eventually the ancestors may be traced to hunter-gatherers using a stone tool technology known as the Hoabinhian. This flaked stone technology, found widely throughout Southeast Asia in caves and shell middens dating back to 12,000 B.C., is characterized by river cobbles flaked along one side only (unifacial flaking). Although unifacial flaking was formerly considered a primitive technology, a study (White and Gorman 1979) of stone artifacts excavated from Tham Pha Chan, northern Thailand, by Gorman in the early 1970s suggests that this flaking technology may have been the best use of locally available raw materials. Sometimes called "Sumatraliths," the core tools (cat. nos. 1–3) could be resharpened until the tool was too small to use, hence "worn out." Many of the flakes recovered from the cave may be byproducts from trimming or resharpening the core tools (cat. nos. 4–8). The steep edge angles of these tools hint that they may have been used for woodworking, which would have necessitated frequent resharpening. Three Hoabinhian cave sites excavated by Gorman in the late 1960s and early '70s produced, in addition to the stone tools, plant remains which suggested that Hoabinhian peoples may have experimented with growing plants.

---

1. **Core Tool** ca. 5000 B.C.
flaked stone
l: 15.3 cm; w: 9.5 cm

---

2 **Core Tool** ca. 5000 B.C.
flaked stone
l: 10.3 cm; w: 5.5 cm

---

3. **Core Tool** ca. 5000 B.C.
flaked stone
l: 8.2 cm; w: 4.4 cm

---

4. **Flake** ca. 5000 B.C.
stone
l: 4.6 cm; w: 4.1 cm

---

5. **Flake** ca. 5000 B.C.
stone
l: 3.9 cm; w: 3.0 cm

---

6. **Flake** ca. 5000 B.C.
stone
l: 3.6 cm; w: 2.2 cm

---

7. **Flake** ca. 5000 B.C.
stone
l: 3.1 cm; w: 2.2 cm

---

8. **Flake** ca. 5000 B.C.
stone
l: 1.8 cm; w: 1.8 cm

---

9. **Hammerstone** ca. 5000 B.C.
stone
l: 8.5 cm; w: 7.1 cm

The heavy chipping on this pebble suggests that it might have been used as a hammerstone to flake the Hoabinhian stone tools.

---

10. **Tool** ca. 5000 B.C.
stone
l: 9.3 cm; w: 6.9 cm

Pecked "doughnut"-like stone rings similar to this one are common in Hoabinhian sites, but their use can only be guessed: two possibilities are digging stick weights or mace heads.

4 5 7

Non Nok Tha, A Prehistoric Site of Northeast Thailand

15

11

11. Digging Stick Tip(?)
ca. 2700 B.C.
copper (?)
l: 9.0 cm; w: 5.3 cm
Burial 90, NNT 152, National Museum of Thailand 99/2525

Nicknamed WOST by fieldworkers for "World's Oldest Socketed Tool," this is the oldest and most enigmatic metal artifact found at Non Nok Tha, and possibly in East Asia. According to one study it may be the only *copper* item known to date among the early metal finds of northeast Thailand (Bayard 1972). Found on the chest of a middle-aged male skeleton, the function of this unique object is unknown, but two have been suggested: either a digging stick tip, or an axe/adze head. The asymmetric socket extending deeply into the tool is curved along one surface and faceted into three planes on the opposing side. The short extension off the end of the socket, which shows possible evidence of hammering, has a longitudinal groove. Controversy over the dating and analysis of this unusual item will be resolved only through further analysis and the accumulation of more supporting data.

12. Axe ca. 2100 B.C.
bronze
l: 6.7 cm; w: 7.1 cm
NP 549

Socketed axes cast in bivalve (two piece) molds, a fairly sophisticated casting technique, are a characteristic tool type for the early bronze tradition of northeast Thailand (cf., cat. no. 94 from Ban Chiang). The analysis of specimens cut from this axe (fig. 42) has shown that the ancient metalsmith had considerable knowledge of the mechanical properties of the alloy bronze. The microstructures show that the edge was heated (annealed) and hammered when cold (cold-worked) in order to strengthen the edge and shape the beautiful lateral splaying. Thus this axe demonstrates an already advanced level of metallurgical production for the early bronze tradition (Smith 1973).

13. Bivalve Axe Mold
ca. 2000 B.C.
sandstone
h: 13.5 cm; w: 9.1 cm
NP 550

14. Bivalve Axe Mold ca. 2000 B.C.
with modern cast
sandstone and bronze
h: 10.7 cm; w: 8.4 cm (mold)
h: 10.2 cm; w: 6.2 cm (axe)
NP 82,a,b, National Museum of Thailand 1236/2524 a, b, and c

The recovery at Non Nok Tha of bivalve molds indicates that bronze items were cast at the site and not merely introduced into the area through trade. The molds were made from local sandstone. A core piece would have been inserted to form the socket. No complete mold sets were excavated at Ban Chiang although some mold fragments were recovered (fig. 56).

15. Pot ca. 2700 B.C.
ceramic
h: 13.8 cm; d: 12.6 cm
NP 522, National Museum of Thailand 1201/2524

Excavations at Non Nok Tha produced not only the first evidence for a Southeast Asian metal-producing tradition, but the first well-documented and dated pottery sequence for the region as well. The ceramic types seemed less spectacular and more standardized than the painted pottery emerging at that time from looters' pits at Ban Chiang. However this vessel with a red-painted curvilinear design on a white background dating to about 2700 B.C. suggested some relationship to the Ban Chiang ware. After scientific excavations took place, the classic painted pottery from Ban Chiang was found to date to about 300 B.C. or later. The presence of red-painted curvilinear designs at the two sites now appears too separated in time to be related. However the holes in the rim and base of this Non Nok Tha painted pot may be compared with the same trait found in Early Period vessels at Ban Chiang (cf., cat. nos. 19, 23).

20

Artifacts of the Ban Chiang Cultural Tradition

16. **Pot** ca. 2000 B.C.
ceramic
h: 14.6 cm; d: 13.8 cm
NNT 377

17. **Pot.** ca. 2000 B.C.
ceramic
h: 11.5 cm; d: 10.5 cm
NP 47,
National Museum of Thailand 123/2516

18. **Pot** ca. 3000 B.C.
ceramic
h: 17.0 cm; d: 15.0 cm
Burial 13, NNT 615

These three examples of pottery from Non Nok Tha illustrate that while the ceramics from this site share general similarities with the Ban Chiang tradition there appears to be little close typological correspondence and some technological distinctions as well. Catalogue number 17, a highly standardized form with unidirectional cord impressions, is the most common funerary pottery, with eighty-seven vessels recovered from the second excavation season burials alone. While nearly identical vessels have been recovered from Don Klang, a site close to Non Nok Tha, no pots of this type have been found at Ban Chiang. Similarly, no Ban Chiang pots compare closely to the red-slipped, polished, and carinated catalogue number 16. Sand temper, while common at Non Nok Tha, is relatively rare at Ban Chiang. In general the Ban Chiang ceramics exhibit greater variety and less standardization of form and decorative treatment which may suggest that Non Nok Tha was somewhat marginal to the creative currents on the prehistoric Khorat Plateau (Bayard 1977).

17

16

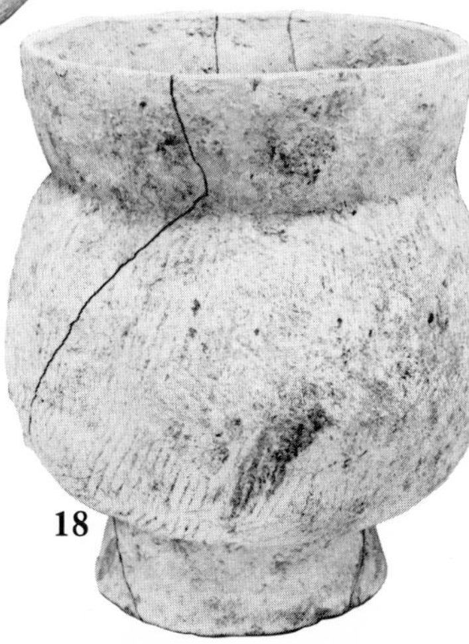

18

Early Period Ceramics of Ban Chiang

19. **Pot** Early Period
ca. 3600–2500 B.C.
ceramic
h: 15.4 cm; d: 13.4 cm
BC 1241 Pot A

20. **Pot** Early Period
ca. 3600–2500 B.C.
ceramic
h: 7.5 cm; d: 10.3 cm
BC 1241 Pot B

The pottery from the basal levels of Ban Chiang contain some of the most elegant and individual forms of the ceramic tradition. The site produced few examples of this oldest pottery so that it is difficult to generalize about the styles, but catalogue number 19 exemplifies the aesthetic sense of the earliest ceramics. The short pedestal base, burnished background, appliqué separating the design field and cordmarked lower body, and small perforations in the rim and base are characteristic of the early pots. These holes might have facilitated stringing up the pot out of reach of rodents and lizards much as contemporary rice baskets are hung between meals. The asymmetrical incised design applied freehand is carefully composed to extend around the pot but does not quite meet. The incised curves are infilled with a back and forth "rocker stamp" pattern which is a design element used in other Early Period pots. The fairly uniform dark hue of this vessel and the small incised pot (cat. no. 20) found close by hint that some control over firing atmosphere might have been achieved. In sum, these early vessels pay tribute to the considerable artistic and technical sophistication of the early inhabitants of Ban Chiang.

19

22 21 23

21. **Pot** Early Period
ca. 3600–2500 B.C.
ceramic
h: 18.8 cm; d: 18.1 cm
Burial 44 Pot A, BC 1339

22. **Pot** Early Period
ca. 3600–2500 B.C.
ceramic
h: 12.9 cm; d: 19.0 cm
Burial 44 Pot B, BC 1339

23. **Pot** Early Period
ca. 3600–2500 B.C.
ceramic
h: 16.3 cm; d: 17.6 cm
Burial 44 Pot C, BC 1339

Since these three vessels (cat. nos. 21–23) were found together as the grave goods placed on the legs of one of the oldest skeletons excavated at Ban Chaing, we know they are contemporaneous. All three have the short foot and ring of appliqué at the midsection characteristic of medium small pots of the early levels. The variable colors of these early unslipped vessels suggest variability in the ancient firing conditions. Since the simple open air firing of local clays today produces a buff to orange product, several examples of grey to black pottery imply deliberate attempts to control oxidation, although conclusive evidence must await technical analyses.

Catalogue number 23 shares many characteristics with catalogue number 19. Both have perforations in the base and rim, possibly to enable suspending the pot by string. Both have burnishing and curious asymmetrical incised designs with rocker stamping infilling. Interestingly, all but one of the five incised arcs on catalogue number 23 face down, the fifth faces up. Examples of such singularity and attention to detail are found throughout the Ban Chaing tradition.

24

24. **Pot** Early Period
ca. 2500–2000 B.C.
ceramic
h: 14.9 cm; d: 14.2 cm
Burial 57 Pot A, BCES 2268

A design element often referred to as rocker stamping is frequently used to fill in space between incised designs in Early Period pots. An implement with a curved edge manipulated in a rocking motion was probably used to impress these tight sawtooth lines around the scroll pattern on the body of this small footed vessel (fig. 35). Very similar design techniques are often found on the shoulders of large pots used for infant burials (e.g., cat. no. 28). Rocker stamping is also used in less busy motifs on the earliest pottery excavated at Ban Chiang (cat. nos. 19, 23), which also shares the perforations in the base and rim. The recurvate rim shape of this pot is highly characteristic of Early Period pots before 2000 B.C.

25. **Pot** Early Period
ca. 2000 B.C.
ceramic
h: 13.2 cm; d: 15.6 cm
Burial 76 Pot A, BCES 2834

Straight-sided pots with short flaring rims and feet are referred to as beaker types and occur only in lower graves of the site. Somewhat uncommon, pots of this style occur in both decorated and undecorated forms. This particular pot is typical of the plainest and simplest form. Fireclouding, its only "decoration," was probably unintentional on the part of the potter. These markings are a product of uneven firing conditions common in a technique where the fuel, possibly straw as is used today, is piled over and around a set of pots and then set aflame. This pot also shows the faint vertical outlines of cordmarking which have been smoothed over. Patchy, crisscrossed cordmarking on the outside of the base and fingerprints on its interior suggest that the base was formed by pressing or pounding it against a flat surface. Faint ridges on the inside of the walls hint at the possibility of coil construction used in combination with paddle and anvil technique.

This pot was found in the grave of a young adult male buried in a crouched or "flexed" position. His grave goods included this pot and one of the excavation's most important finds, a socketed spearhead (cat. no. 92), one of the oldest bronze artifacts from a grave at the site (fig. 43).

26. **Pot** Early Period
ca. 2000–1600 B.C.
ceramic
h: 14.8 cm; d: 18.1 cm
Burial 52 Pot A, BCES 2208

This beaker type pot is the most elaborately decorated of those found at Ban Chiang. Its flange is attached near the base, typical of other beakers. However the red pigment covering most of the exterior is extremely unusual not only for the beaker style but for the entire period, becoming common only during the later periods. Freely painted vertical stripes on the pot interior also presage the Late Period ceramics, when freehand painting becomes the norm. This beaker pot was placed at the feet of a child, about six years old, along with several other pots of plainer design and possibly more utilitarian use.

27. **Pot** Early Period
ca. 2000–1600 B.C.
ceramic
h: 18.6 cm; d: 20.4 cm
Burial 38 Pot A, BCES 1983

Pots whose predominate surface decoration is cord impressions are found throughout the Ban Chiang sequence and in fact characterize the prehistoric ceramic tradition all over Southeast Asia. The cord impressions on these pots were applied by either striking the surface with a cord-wrapped paddle or by rolling a cord-wrapped stick down the sides of the vessel. This pot shows evidence of both kinds of application. The upper half of the pot has rolled cordmarking applied in wide vertical bands, while the lower half shows the typical crisscross pattern of paddled cordmarking. The bases of these pots are almost always covered with such cordmarking, probably because the action of paddling helped form the round base of the pot. Paddling also strengthened the pot walls by compacting the clay and removing air bubbles.

This particular pot has an extended vertical neck which is typical of the many plain round pots from the Early Period (cf., cat. no. 32). It was found at the head of a five-year-old child wearing bronze anklets (cat. no. 93) that are some of the earliest examples of bronze jewelry recovered at Ban Chiang.

28. **Burial Jar** (Fragment) Early Period ca. 3000–2000 B.C.
ceramic
h:16.5 cm; d:44.5 cm
Burial 40 Pot A, BC 1205

27

26

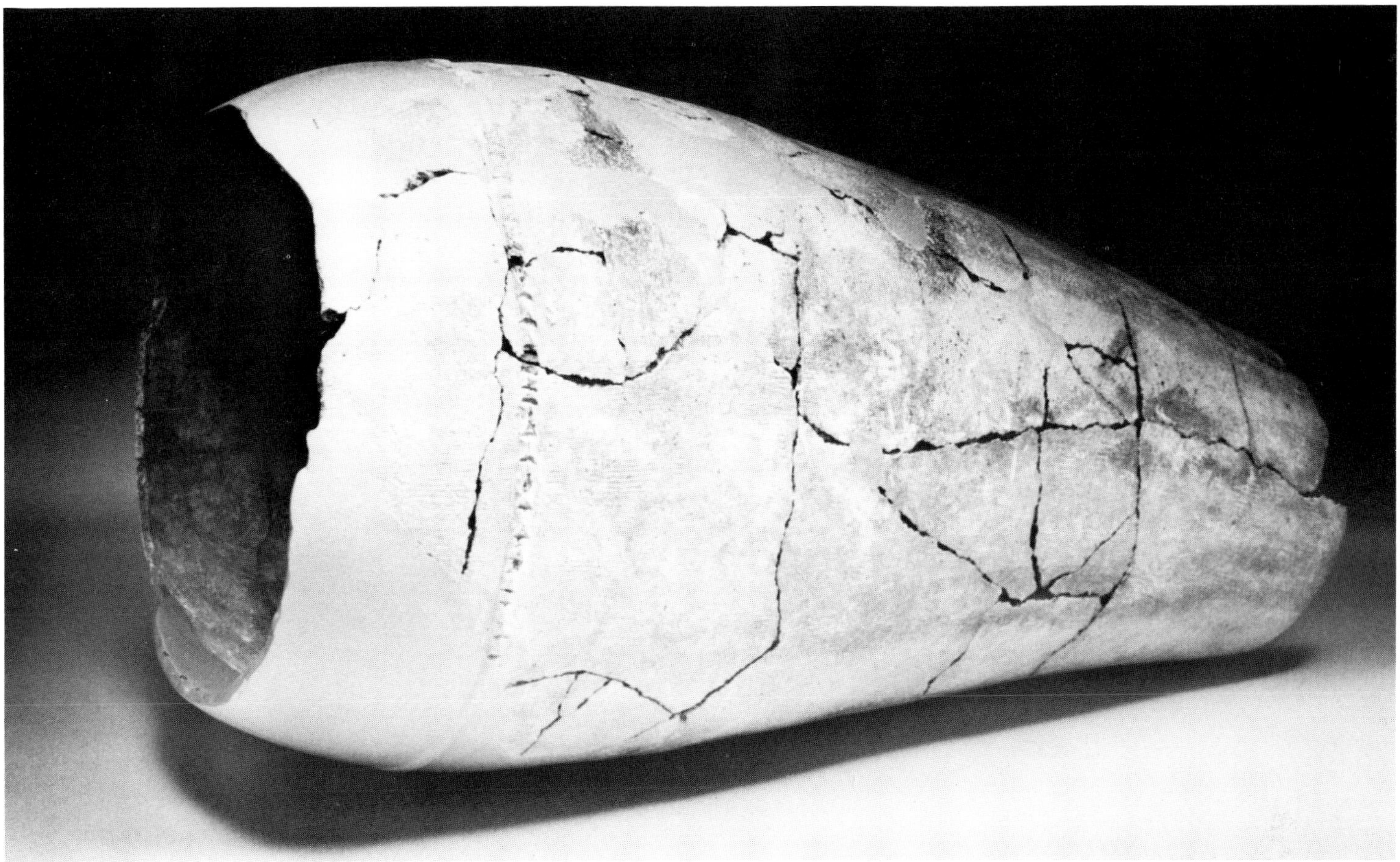

30

29. **Cup** Early Period
ca. 3000–2000 B.C.
ceramic
h: 5.7 cm; d: 7.1 cm
Burial 40 Pot B, BC 1335

Several large vessels of the Early Period found placed on their sides contained skeletons of very young humans. Although they ranged in age from a seven-month-old fetus to a two-year-old child, the majority were at most a few weeks old. The earliest type of infant burial jar (fig. 24, cat. no. 28) found prior to 2000 B.C. has an intricate scroll design of curvilinear incising and punctated rocker stamping on the shoulder of the vessel. A thin raised band (appliqué) separates the design field from the cord impressed lower body. This style of dense *horror vacui* incising, while characteristic of the earliest burial jars, is occasionally found on smaller pots as well (cat. no. 24). The decorative technique may be a stylistic development from less densely incised pots (cat. nos. 19, 23). Only the sections of this pot revealed in the excavation were recovered; the remainder, embedded in the side wall of the pit, was left *in situ*. The plain cup (cat. no. 29) found just below the large pot might have contained food or other offerings for the two-year-old child.

30. **Burial Jar** Early Period
ca. 2000–1500 B.C.
ceramic
h: 64.5 cm; d: 34.4 cm
Burial 77, BCES 2837

31. **Burial Jar** Early Period
ca. 2000–1500 B.C.
ceramic
h: 36.0 cm; d: 30.8 cm
Burial 64, BCES 2358

32. **Burial Jar** Early Period
ca. 1500 B.C.
ceramic
h: 44.5 cm; d: 40.3 cm
Burial 48, BCES 2100

Infant burial jars of the second millennium B.C. have simple decoration. An elongate vessel with appliqué on the shoulder has red-painted bands faintly visible along the longitudinal axis (cat. no. 30). One cord impressed jar has a "serpentine" appliqué also found on many incised pots of the Early Period (cat. no. 31). Catalogue number 32 has a tall neck over a globular cord-impressed body. Generally these pots are missing their bases and sometimes their rims, which were perhaps purposely broken off as part of the burial ritual.

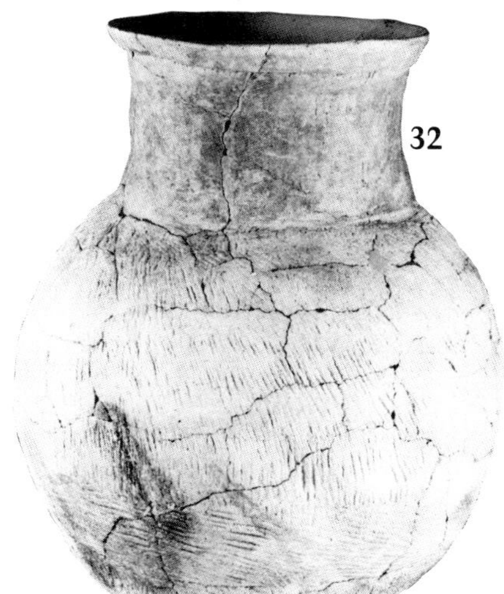

32

33. **Pot** Early Period
ca. 1600–1000 B.C.
ceramic
h: 21.8 cm; d: 23.5 cm
Burial 33 Pot A, BCES 1722

Toward the end of the Early Period, many elements transitional to the Middle Period appeared. People were still buried in the style of earlier phases: supine with one or more whole pots placed at the foot or head. But the orientation shifted from a northwest-southeast axis to an east-west axis. The pottery shapes of these early burials with an east-west orientation are distinctive and relatively standardized. Footless, round bottomed, globular, and cordmarked vessels predominate, and painted decoration on the upper body and rim becomes increasingly common. The rims usually flare straight out from the shoulder. Little is known about the everyday functions of Ban Chiang ceramics since most were recovered from funerary contexts and show few signs of wear. However the size and shape of these vessels are comparable to pots made in the Ban Chiang region today for steaming rice or cooking soups. Some of the funerary pots did contain rice, fish, or other animal bones presumably as food offerings.

Catalogue number 33 is a very early example of the type. It has a characteristic flared rim. The body surface exhibits a particularly beautiful example of paddled cordmarking. This cordmarking, which was applied with great care and clarity, demonstrates how cordmarking can be a product of both a manufacturing technique and of a decorative impulse. Striking the vessel with a cordwrapped paddle compacted and strengthened the clay walls, and in this case the resultant imprints achieved a decorative patchwork effect as well. The clarity of the imprints is such that the twist of the original cords can be clearly seen. This pot was found intact at the feet of a young adult female.

33

34. **Pot** Early Period
ca. 1300–1000 B.C.
ceramic
h: 19.0 cm; d: 21.0 cm
BC 1630

35. **Pot** Early Period
ca. 1600–1300 B.C.
ceramic
h: 10.7 cm; d: 16.5 cm
Burial 23, BC 1203

Toward the end of the Early Period globular cordmarked pots with red-painted and incised designs on the shoulders appeared. This style is sometimes called Om Kaeo after a site about one kilometer from Ban Chiang which produced many examples. The designs are often in the curvilinear scroll type pattern which is found throughout the sequence, but geometric patterns such as sawtooth are also common. During the Middle Period larger, often carinated, pots carry similar decorative treatment (cat. no. 42). Catalogue number 35 (fig. 51) was found at the foot of a very distinctive burial, a middle-aged male referred to by the excavators as "Vulcan." The burial also had four bronze bracelets (cat. no. 95), a socketed bronze adze (cat. no. 94), and about thirty pellets (cat. no. 36), possibly for use with the pellet bow for hunting small mammals.

36

36. **Pellets** Early Period
ca. 1600–1300 B.C.
ceramic
d: 2.0 cm (ave.)
Burial 23, BC SF 2103/1203

Except for pottery sherds, the most common ceramic artifacts encountered at the site were small spherical baked clay balls referred to as pellets. Although most pellets came from nonspecific contexts, the unusual Early Period burial of the male referred to as "Vulcan" contained a pile of about thirty pellets just to the upper right of his skull. The probable use of these items would be a mystery but for the survival until recent times of a weapon called the pellet bow (cat. no. 176). Although the bow is no longer employed in the Ban Chiang vicinity, elderly men who as children used the weapon to hunt small animals or to herd water buffalo can still make these bows. The distinguishing feature of the pellet bow is a split string with a tiny platform woven from rattan at the midsection. Round objects can be grasped against this platform and propelled in the usual manner of handling a long bow. Such a use is presently the best, though not the only, possible interpretation for the ubiquitous pellets found at Ban Chiang.

34

Middle Period Ceramics of Ban Chiang

37. Pot Middle Period ca. 1000 B.C.
ceramic
h: 41.6 cm; d: 52.2 cm
Burial 17 Pot D, BC 900

The funerary pottery from the Middle Period demonstrates impressive developments in ceramic craftsmanship. Potters experimented with large yet extraordinarily light forms. By maintaining thin walls, they created vessels whose scuptural elegance is unequaled in any other period. These ceramic types were virtually unknown prior to careful excavation and reconstruction by archaeologists. Their former obscurity was most likely due to the grave ritual common during the Middle Period. These large pots seem to have been purposely broken over the bodies, often several pots per grave. Since looters have generally sought intact pottery, the broken sherds of these superb pots from this period were largely ignored.

This pot was broken over a middle-aged man. Only half of it was recovered since the burial lay only partially within the excavation square, and standard archaeological practice requires the remainder of the pot be left undisturbed in the unexcavated deposit.

The stylistic relationship of this large vessel to the smaller, plain, round, cordmarked vessels from the Early Period can be seen in its simple spherical shape, flared straight rim, and thin line of red paint around the rim edge (cf., cat. nos. 33, 34). However, its size, delicate surface decoration, and the uniform thinness of the walls are strikingly different from its antecedents. Fine, stylized incising and meticulous use of red paint demonstrate extreme care in execution. The rolled cord impressions show that a thin, delicate cord was employed, as if to harmonize with the delicacy of the incising.

38. Pot Middle Period ca. 1000 B.C.
ceramic
h: 34.2 cm; d: 39.1 cm
Burial 18 Pot A, BC 712

Although this vessel is similar to catalogue number 37, its cordmarking, incising, and painting are perhaps even more finely executed. The physical shape of this pot is of particular stylistic interest. Its gently angled profile may be a formal precedent to the sharply defined angles referred to as carinations found on pots in the later Middle Period.

39. Pot Middle Period
ca. 1000–400 B.C.
ceramic
h: 49.0 cm; d: 40.8 cm
Burial 40 Pot A, BCES 1934

37

39

38

40. **Pot** Middle Period
ca. 1000–400 B.C.
ceramic
h: 13.1 cm; d: 35.7 cm
Burial 40 Pot F, BCES 1717

41. **Pot** Middle Period
ca. 1000–400 B.C.
ceramic
h: 37.2 cm; d: 42.5 cm
Burial 40 Pot H, BCES 1929

40

During the Middle Period an unusual style of burial containing highly distinctive ceramics was uncovered. Excavators came down upon sheets of sherds spread over human skeletons. For most examples no grave cut could be defined, as though the bodies had been placed on the ground surface with sherds then spread over the bodies. Earth might have been mounded over the top. After months of work in the basement of the University Museum, the lab crew reconstructed several pots for each sherd sheet. The pots are generally of two types with some variation within each type. For burial 40, which contained a middle-aged male uncovered during the 1975 excavation season, seven white carinated pots with simple red-painted trim under the rim were distinguished. Five of these were of the short variety (e.g., cat. no. 41) and two were of the statuesque, tall variety (cat. no. 39). In addition to these seven, two of the red-painted and incised carinated Om Kaeo ware were reconstructed (cat. no. 40). The similarity in sizes and styles gives the impression that they were chosen as a "set" rather than a random assortment of whatever pots were available. Interestingly, the man found in burial 40 wore a matched pair of bracelets of the distinctive flanged style: one of bronze (cat. no. 103) and one of calcite (cat. no. 140).

42. **Pot** Middle Period
ca. 800–400 B.C.
ceramic
h: 29.0 cm; d: 32.5 cm
D7 Scatter Pot I, BCES 1048

Some Middle Period burials covered by sherd sheets may have contained two or more individuals. These carinated pots (cat. nos. 42, 43, 44) came from a possible multiple grave of such complexity and disturbance that it is uncertain how many individuals were included in it. Although several skeletons were incomplete, it appears that the individuals were of varied age and sex, thus leading the excavators to think that the group may have comprised a family.

Like the skeletal remains in this grave complex, the ceramic remains were in a confused and disturbed state. Nevertheless, during reconstruction it was determined that, as in other scatter burials, the pot types included a mix of both the white carinated wares (cat. nos. 43, 44) and large red-painted and incised carinated wares (fig. 28, cat. no. 42). The

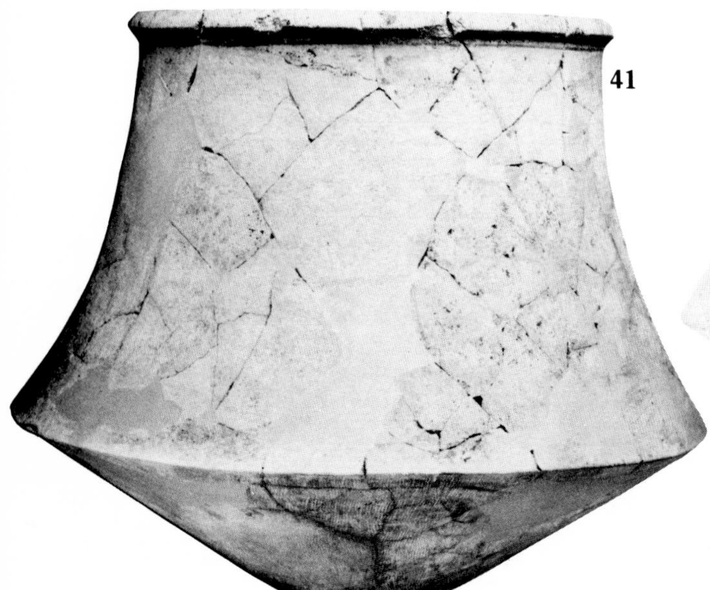

41

43

curvilinear incising and painting on the upper shoulder of these latter, often ruddy-hued, pots is generally more finely executed than comparable designs on smaller pots from the late Early Period (cf., cat. nos. 34, 35).

43. **Pot** Middle Period
ca. 800–400 B.C.
ceramic
h: 26.7 cm; d: 38.0 cm
D7 Scatter Pot A, BCES 1040

Marks on the interior walls of the large Middle Period vessels have left clues as to how these thin pots were constructed. A seam at the midsection or carination is usually evident, indicating a multistage or compound manufacturing process. It is likely that the bases, especially those with concave contours, were paddled on molds made of wood or perhaps on the base of another pot. Use of molds would have fostered a standardization of forms which is increasingly notable for the Middle Period. The smooth upper body could have been added after the molded section had partially dried. This might have been accomplished by the coil or slab method. Imprints of anvils on the interior indicate that the pots were paddled to promote bonding and to shape the final contours.

44. **Pot** Middle Period
ca. 800–400 B.C.
ceramic
h: 33.5 cm; d: 29.2 cm
D7 Scatter Pot K, BCES 1040

The rather unwieldy, though graceful, shapes of the carinated vessels have raised questions as to whether the objects were utilitarian or were intended only for funerary use. The shattered condition of most of these pots points to ritual use, but faint signs of wear on this pot suggest that at least some pots may have been used prior to "sacrifice." A light band of abrasion on the lower half of this pot suggests that it may have been set in a ring of some sort which enabled it to stand upright and to possibly hold stored food (fig. 16).

45

45. **Pot** Middle Period
ca. 400–300 B.C.
ceramic
h: 36.5 cm; d: 39.2 cm
Burial 12 Pot B, BCES 1010

This distinctive pot, referred to as a carabel type, is one of four nearly identical vessels from the grave of a one-year-old child. In addition, three nearly identical carinated pots were also reconstructed with a rim type matching the carabel ware. In contrast to the preceding scatter burials, for which apparently no grave was dug, the orientation of the sherds over this burial indicated that the body had been interred in a grave several centimeters deep (fig. 29).

The latest of the Middle Period types, the carabel pots are unique to this particular grave, and the four vessels are so similar in size and construction that they were almost certainly made by a single potter, possibly using a single mold. Although the walls are still thin, the rather heavy rim and solid red paint suggest a trend toward the more substantial pottery of the Late Period. The paddled cord imprints on the base are also noticeably coarser than preceding styles.

The abundance of this young child's grave goods is striking and suggests that the child was given a burial comparable to an adult. This might indicate that social status was inherited, and that the Ban Chiang society of this period may have had a class structure.

46. **Ladle** Middle Period
ca. 1000–300 B.C.
ceramic
l: 20.4 cm; w: 11.4 cm
Burial 27, BC SF 2040/1114

Although many clay ladle handles were found in the deposits at Ban Chiang, this is the only complete ladle recovered. It is from the burial of a middle-aged male.

46

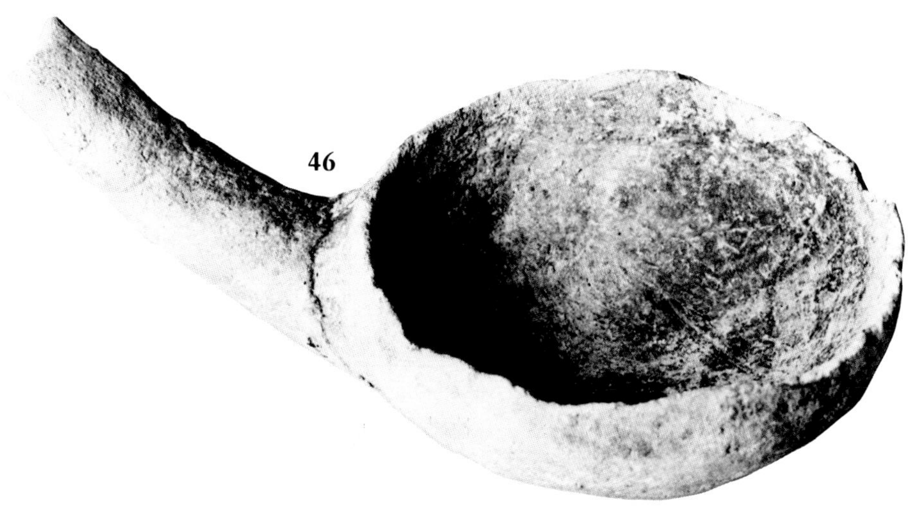

50 49 47

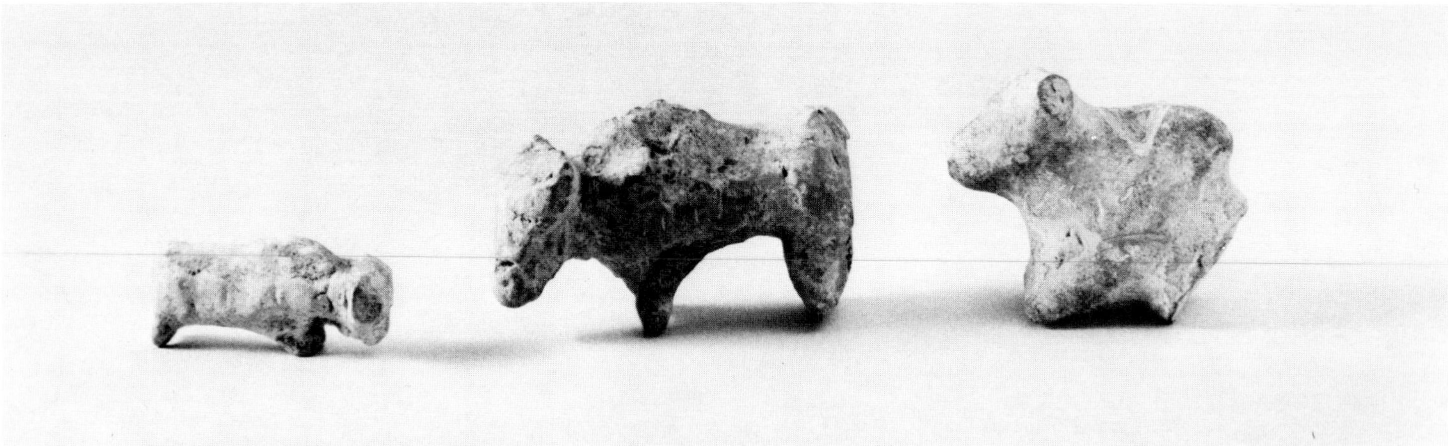

47. **Figurine** Late Period
ca. 300 B.C.–A.D. 200
ceramic
l: 5.0 cm; w: 2.3 cm
BCES SF 361/1002

48. **Figurine** Middle Period
ca. 1000–300 B.C.
ceramic
l: 5.7 cm; w: 1.8 cm
BCES SF 420/1206

49. **Figurine** Middle Period
ca. 1000–300 B.C.
ceramic
l: 6.1 cm; w. 2.5 cm
Burial 40, BCES SF 583/1896

50. **Figurine** ca. 1500 B.C.
ceramic
l: 4.1 cm; w: 1.4 cm
BPT SF 17/S69

Representations of natural forms are notably rare in the Ban Chiang cultural tradition, though it is, of course, possible that living things were depicted in perishable materials such as wood. Nonetheless, a few simple baked clay animal figurines have been recovered from Ban Chiang and related sites. Most of these appear to be of humped cattle (e.g., cat. nos. 47, 49, 50), a genus whose skeletal remains are found throughout the site. Catalogue number 48 is a likely example of a water buffalo (fig. 31). That primarily the large bovids were considered suitable to depict is interesting considering the great diversity of animal species large and small, hunted and bred, which were exploited by the ancient peoples. Thus the cattle figurines may reflect their ideological significance more than their economic role.

51. **Crucible** Middle Period
ca. 1000 B.C.
ceramic
l: 8.8 cm; h: 4.5 cm
BCES SF 419/1205

52. **Crucible** Middle Period
ca. 1000 B.C.
ceramic
l: 11.6 cm; h: 6.0 cm
BCES SF 760/2826

53. **Crucible** Middle Period
ca. 1000–300 B.C.
ceramic
l: 10.1 cm; h: 5.2 cm
GC #1

The presence of the clay crucibles and the sandstone molds in Ban Chiang culture sites shows that casting took place at these sites, and that the bronze items found there were not imported trade goods. Catalogue number 52 shows probable use as a vessel for melting and alloying bronze. Impurities from the ingots or ores coagulated during the melting process and adhered to the crucible when the bronze was poured off into the mold. These impurities left dross visible on the interior walls. Red staining may be due to an iron-based impurity, or to the purposeful addition of hematite to promote the separation of impurities from the bronze alloy. The crucibles contain a high percentage of rice chaff in the fabric. It has been proposed that the silica in the rice husks helped to prevent the fracturing of the crucible from the intense heat (about 1083 degrees C to melt copper). The unburnt exteriors of the crucibles suggest that the fuel (charcoal) used to heat the metals was probably placed on top of the crucible (fig. 47).

53

Late Period Ceramics of Ban Chiang

54

54. Pot Late Period
ca. 300 B.C.–A.D. 1
ceramic
h: 16.0 cm; d: 15.8 cm
Burial 23/11 Pot B, BCES 1390

Pottery with painted swirling designs first brought attention to the site of Ban Chiang. This pot is the most beautiful and pristine example of this style excavated by the NETAP excavations at the site. The parallel meander design bounded by the neck and pedestal is a somewhat uncommon motif and was carefully composed and painted freehand. Despite the careful planning of the pattern, a slight miscalculation can be observed in the overlap of two lines on the foot.

55

56

55. **Pot** Late Period
ca. 300 B.C.–A.D. 1
ceramic
h: 34.8 cm; d: 33.7 cm
Burial 23/11 Pot A, BCES 1426

This large globular pot with slightly flared rim was found immediately adjacent to another pot (cat. no. 54). Decorated around the rim with a simple linear zigzag, the restraint of the design demonstrates contemporaneity of fairly plain vessels with the better known baroque types. Burnishing, possibly produced by rubbing the pot with a smooth stone while the vessel was leather hard, covers most of the exterior.

56. **Pot** Late Period
ca. 300 B.C.–A.D. 1
ceramic
h: 36.1 cm; d: 27.7 cm
Burial 9 Pot D, BCES 700

Although the freehand-painted designs of much of the classic Ban Chiang painted pottery have fascinated viewers with the creativity and complexity of their compositions, many vessels are rather crudely built and fired. This may be a function of their nonutilitarian, funerary role. Also, as in any artistic movement, many trials and failures may be produced before a masterpiece is created. This vessel with interlocking "S" curves around the upper body was found with several other pots in a well-appointed grave of a middle-aged female. During the Late Period pots were placed over the grave intact, though in time they often collapsed in place from the weight of the surrounding soil.

57

58

57. **Pot** Late Period
ca. 200 B.C.–A.D. 200
ceramic
h: 35.7 cm; d: 29.7 cm
Burial 7 Pot A, BCES 813

Pottery made somewhat later than the classic red-on-buff styles often have similarly complex red-painted designs against an orange or red background. Although the painted patterns exhibit highly diverse combinations of motifs, vessel shapes tend to be standardized to a few types. This well-made pedestalled vessel with broad flaring rim was encountered in the well-furnished grave of an elderly male, along with several other pots plus iron tools and weapons. In the pots and around the grave were scattered many chicken bones, possibly offerings made during the burial ritual.

58. **Pot** Late Period
ca. 200 B.C.–A.D. 200
ceramic
h: 28.7 cm; d: 31.4 cm
Burial 13 Pot A, BCES 1086

This style of pot, characteristic of the Late Period, has a wide flaring rim and a lustrous burnished surface. It is found in graves with red pots with red-painted designs (e.g. cat. no. 57). This one was placed with five other pots in a well-furnished grave of an eighteen-month-old child. Also discovered in this interesting burial were four rollers (cat. nos. 77, 78, 79, 80) and a disarticulated skeleton of a dog. The skull of the dog was placed in one bowl, the vertebrae and ribs in a pot, and the remaining bones over the child's chest.

60

61

59

---

59. **Pot** Late Period
ca. 200 B.C.–A.D. 200
ceramic
h: 41.9 cm; d: 29.8 cm
Burial 8 Pot A, BCES 857

---

60. **Pot** Late Period
ca. 200 B.C.–A.D. 200
ceramic
h: 14.3 cm; d: 20.4 cm
Burial 8 Pot B, BCES 857

---

61. **Pot** Late Period
ca. 200 B.C.–A.D. 200
ceramic
h: 36.8 cm; d: 30.4 cm
Burial 8 Pot C, BCES 857

The Late Period grave of a three-year-old child contained these three pots (cat. nos. 59–61) placed over the body and four baked clay rollers (cat. nos. 73–76) placed at the feet. The spiral red-painted designs of catalogue number 59 show stylistic continuity from earlier red-on-buff styles. The red-painted and burnished exteriors of catalogue numbers 60 and 61 are also characteristic of the Late Period. The thick walls yielded sturdy though heavy vessels which contrast with the often rather delicate ceramics of earlier periods. The size, shape, and strength of the bowl (cat. no. 60) suggest that it might have had a utilitarian as well as funerary role.

Late Period Rollers of Ban Chiang

---

62. **Roller** Late Period
ca. 200 B.C.–A.D. 200
ceramic
l: 5.3 cm; d: 2.3 cm
BC SF 51/275

---

63. **Roller** Late Period
ca. 200 B.C.–A.D. 200
ceramic
l: 5.5 cm; d: 4.3 cm
BC SF 70/437

---

64. **Roller** Late Period
ca. 200 B.C.–A.D. 200
ceramic
l: 6.1 cm; d: 3.0 cm
BC SF 80/691

---

65. **Roller** Late Period
ca. 200 B.C.–A.D. 200
ceramic
l: 4.7 cm; d: 2.8 cm
Burial 14, BC SF 2171/881

---

66. **Roller** Late Period
ca. 200 B.C.–A.D. 200
ceramic
l: 4.1 cm; d: 3.0 cm
Burial 14, BC SF 2173/881

---

67. **Roller** Late Period
ca. 200 B.C.–A.D. 200
ceramic
l: 5.9 cm; d: 4.1 cm
Burial 14, BC SF 2174/881

---

68. **Roller** Late Period
ca. 200 B.C.–A.D. 200
ceramic
l: 7.6 cm; d: 2.5 cm
BCES SF 192/313

72 75 77 71

69. **Roller** Late Period
ca. 200 B.C.–A.D. 200
ceramic
l: 6.1 cm; d: 2.4 cm
BCES SF 211/392

70. **Roller** Late Period
ca. 200 B.C.–A.D. 200
ceramic
l: 5.8 cm; d: 2.7 cm
BCES SF 212/417

71. **Roller** Late Period
ca. 200 B.C.–A.D. 200
ceramic
l: 7.3 cm; d: 2.8 cm
BCES SF 257/629

72. **Roller** Late Period
ca. 200 B.C.–A.D. 200
ceramic
l: 6.9 cm; d: 3.0 cm
Burial 4, BCES SF 267/537

73. **Roller** Late Period
ca. 200 B.C.–A.D. 200
ceramic
l: 6.3 cm; d: 2.8 cm
Burial 8, BCES SF 313/857

74. **Roller** Late Period
ca. 200 B.C.–A.D. 200
ceramic
l: 4.3 cm; d: 4.2 cm
Burial 8, BCES SF 314/857

75. **Roller** Late Period
ca. 200 B.C.–A.D. 200
ceramic
l: 4.2 cm; d: 2.7 cm
Burial 8, BCES SF 315/857

76. **Roller** Late Period
ca. 200 B.C.–A.D. 200
ceramic
l: 6.0 cm; d: 2.9 cm
Burial 8, BCES SF 320/857

77. **Roller** Late Period
ca. 200 B.C.–A.D. 200
ceramic
l: 6.2 cm; d: 3.0 cm
Burial 13, BCES SF 368/1021

78. **Roller** Late Period
ca. 200 B.C.–A.D. 200
ceramic
l: 4.2 cm; d: 3.1 cm
Burial 13, BCES SF 369/1021

79. **Roller** Late Period
ca. 200 B.C.–A.D. 200
ceramic
l: 4.6 cm; d: 2.6 cm
Burial 13, BCES SF 370/1021

80. **Roller** Late Period
ca. 200 B.C.–A.D. 200
ceramic
l: 6.2 cm; d: 3.1 cm
Burial 13, BCES SF 393/1106

81. **Roller** Late Period
ca. 200 B.C.–A.D. 200
ceramic
l: 6.2 cm; d: 3.0 cm
BCES SF 732/2561

In the upper levels of the Ban Chiang site ceramic cylinders with deeply carved designs and a hole through the longitudinal axis were found both within and outside of the burials (fig. 54). Although there is little direct evidence for their function, the most frequently suggested use for these curious objects is textile printing. The printing technique might have been a relief or stenciling method similar to that used by Pacific Islanders to print bark cloth (van Esterik and Kress 1978). The variety and intricacy of many designs echo the patterning of the painted pottery of the same time period, but there is no evidence that the rollers were used to apply the decoration to the pottery. The carved patterns yield simple linear designs (cat. nos. 63, 67, 70, 73, 74, 75), zigzags (cat. nos. 65, 66, 77, 78, 79), geometric designs (cat. nos. 62, 68, 69, 72), and curvilinear designs (cat. nos. 64, 71, 76, 80, 81). Noteworthy is the fact that some quite elaborate designs are almost exactly duplicated (cat. nos. 71 and 155; cat. nos. 76 and 80). Since the manufacture and use of these implements must have required considerable skill, the placement of rollers with children aged one to six years old, too young to have been accomplished artisans, seems significant. No adult burials yielded rollers. The reason for this practice is unknown.

82

82. Spindle Whorl Middle Period
ca. 1000–300 B.C.
ceramic
l: 2.0 cm; w: 3.0 cm
BCES SF 418/1203

83. Spindle Whorl ca. A.D. 1–100
ceramic
l: 2.4 cm; w: 3.2 cm
DK SF 121/S312

84. Spindle Whorl ca. A.D. 1–100
ceramic
l: 1.6 cm; w: 3.0 cm
DK SF 337/S561

85. Spindle Whorl ca. A.D. 1–100
ceramic
l: 2.7 cm; w: 3.3 cm
DK SF 338/S561

Although the function of these perforated, semispherical ceramic objects found at Ban Chiang and related sites is not really known, they are sometimes interpreted as spindle whorls. The few examples recovered at Ban Chiang were from mid to upper layers, overlapping the distribution of the rollers (cat. nos. 62–81) which might have been used for textile printing. The fibers used for the woven textiles which occasionally survive in the archaeological record have not yet been identified. However, aboriginal tribes of Taiwan which may be distantly related to mainland Southeast Asian peoples have used spindle whorls to twist ramie yarn, prior to the introduction of cotton (Chi-Lu 1968: 101).

86. Anvil Late Period
ca. 300 B.C.–A.D. 200
ceramic
l: 13.2 cm; w: 7.6 cm
BC SF 2039/716

87. Anvil Late Period
ca. 300 B.C.–A.D. 200
ceramic
l: 6.4 cm; w: 5.1 cm
BCES SF 150/183

88. Anvil ca. 1000–300 B.C.
ceramic
l: 4.8 cm; w: 5.8 cm
BT SF 500/S930

89. Anvil age unknown
ceramic
l: 12.1 cm; w: 8.1 cm
BPT SF 405

While these mushroom-shaped baked clay objects might have been used as pestles to grind food or other substances, very similar items are employed today in northeast Thailand as anvils in pottery manufacture (cat. nos. 179–81). An anvil is used to support the inside wall of a pot while the exterior is beaten with a wooden paddle to shape the walls and compact the clay. The shape and size of the anvil depend on the desired size of the pot. This paddle and anvil technique of pottery manufacture is found traditionally throughout Southeast Asia, and marks on prehistoric pottery indicate that the technique has been in use for thousands of years in the region. While potters in the Ban Chiang area use clay anvils, potters of other regions sometimes use smooth stones. The use of baked clay anvils in the ethnographic and prehistoric records of this region may be due to the dearth of suitable stone resources.

90. Beads Late Period
ca. 300 B.C.–A.D. 200
glass
l: 9.5 cm
Burial 14, BC SF 2139/918

91. Bead Necklace Late Period
ca. 300 B.C.–A.D. 200
glass
l: 51.2 cm
Burial 5, BCES SF 1186/733

Although beads reputedly from Ban Chiang culture sites are prominent items in the antiquities trade, few beads were unearthed during scientific excavations at Ban Chiang. However, two Late Period burials of children aged five to seven years did contain orangy-red glasslike beads which appear to have been sliced off cylindrical tubes. The series of close to 200 beads from one burial also contained a few blue and yellow translucent glass beads (cat. no. 91). Although little is known about how or where these beads were made, the development of glass beadmaking in other parts of the world is associated with the development of iron technology.

89 88 87

91 90

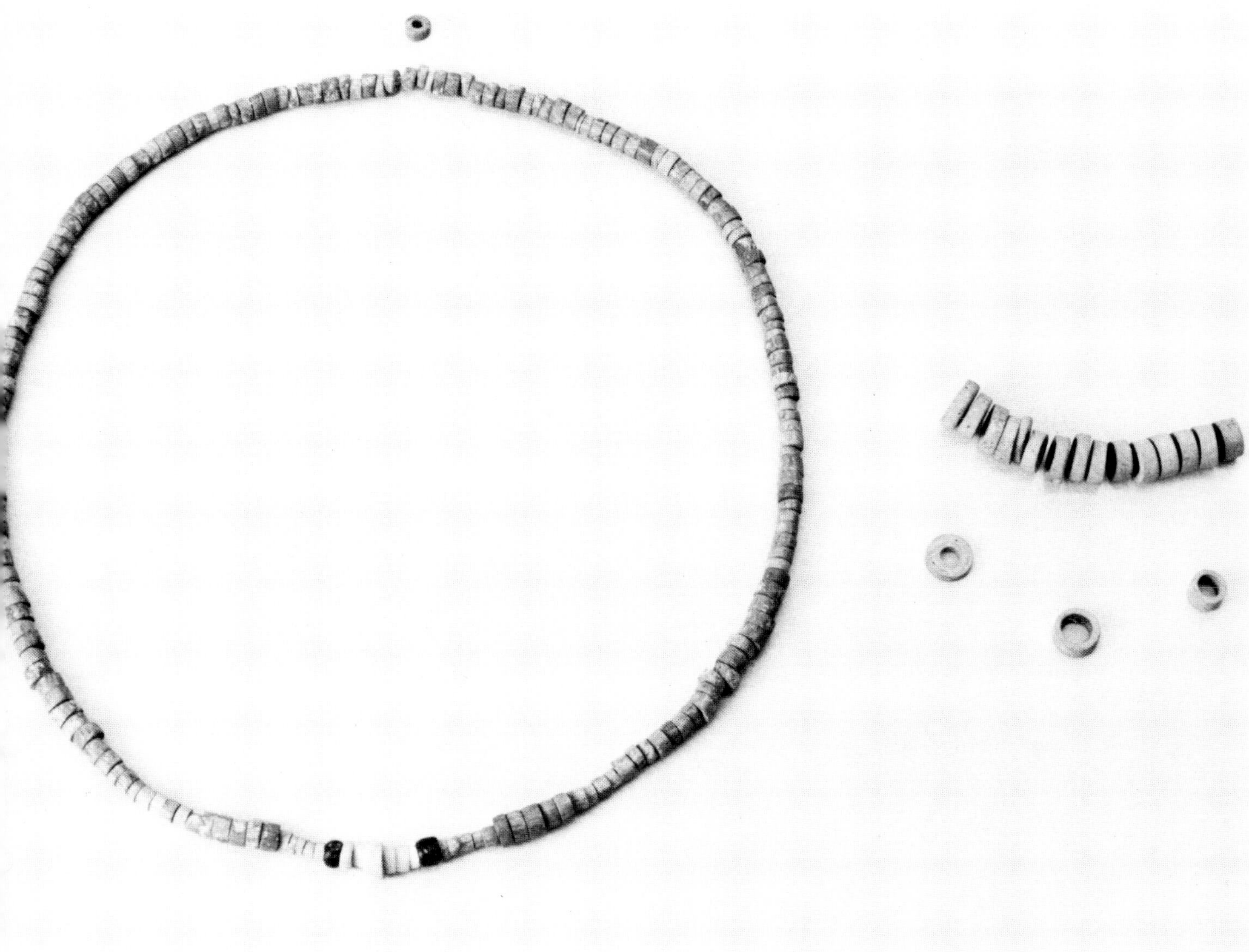

Metal Artifacts of Ban Chiang

92. **Spearpoint** Early Period
ca. 2000 B.C.
bronze
l: 13.6 cm; w: 3.8 cm
Burial 76, BCES SF 762/2834

This socketed bronze spearpoint is from the deepest levels and is one of the oldest bronze artifacts recovered from a grave during the NETAP excavations at Ban Chiang. It was uncovered in a flexed burial of a young adult male at the end of the 1975 season just before the side walls of the excavation threatened to collapse over the pit. The conservator of the piece determined that the tip had been bent prior to interment, as though the object had been purposely mutilated. An unpretentious beaker pot (fig. 43, cat. no. 25) had also been placed in the grave.

Scientific analysis of a sample cut from the blade indicated that this spearpoint is a product of considerable technological sophistication. Although the percentage of tin is small, about 1.3 percent, the ancient metalsmith employed reheating and hammering to strengthen the edge. Furthermore, the casting technique used, with a two-piece mold and a core piece inserted to form the socket, is far beyond rudimentary requirements to produce a sharp weapon.

93. **Anklets** Early Period
ca. 2000–1600 B.C.
bronze
d: 6.5 cm (ave.)
Burial 38, BCES SF 594, 595, 596/1984

Bronzes from the Early Period include ornamental bangles as well as tools. These plain bronze anklets were found in a low burial of a five-year-old child at whose head was placed a cordmarked pot (cat. no. 27). Such prestigious items buried with a child not yet old enough to have attained high status through personal achievement imply that status may be inherited, even during the Early Period. However, it might also indicate that the child was particularly cherished by parents who had accumulated some wealth.

94. **Adze** Early Period
ca. 1600–1300 B.C.
bronze
l: 8.9 cm; w: 6.9 cm
Burial 23, BC SF 694/1203

95. **Bracelets** Early Period
ca. 1600–1300 B.C.
bronze
d: 7.2 cm
Burial 23, BC SF 693/1203

An unusual burial of a middle-aged man was called "Vulcan" by the excavators due to the singularity of his grave goods, in particular the prominence of bronze objects (fig. 25, 50, 51). These goods included four bronze bracelets on his left arm (cat. no. 95), a bronze adze (cat. no. 94) at his left shoulder, a pile of clay pellets to the upper right of his skull (cat. no. 36), and a painted and incised pot at his feet (cat. no. 35). Analysis of the edge of the socketed adze showed no signs of hammering or heating as has been found on other bivalve mold-cast implements from Ban Chiang (cat. no. 92) and Non Nok Tha (cat. no. 12). The lack of such treatment for this item may mean that it was never utilized prior to interment.

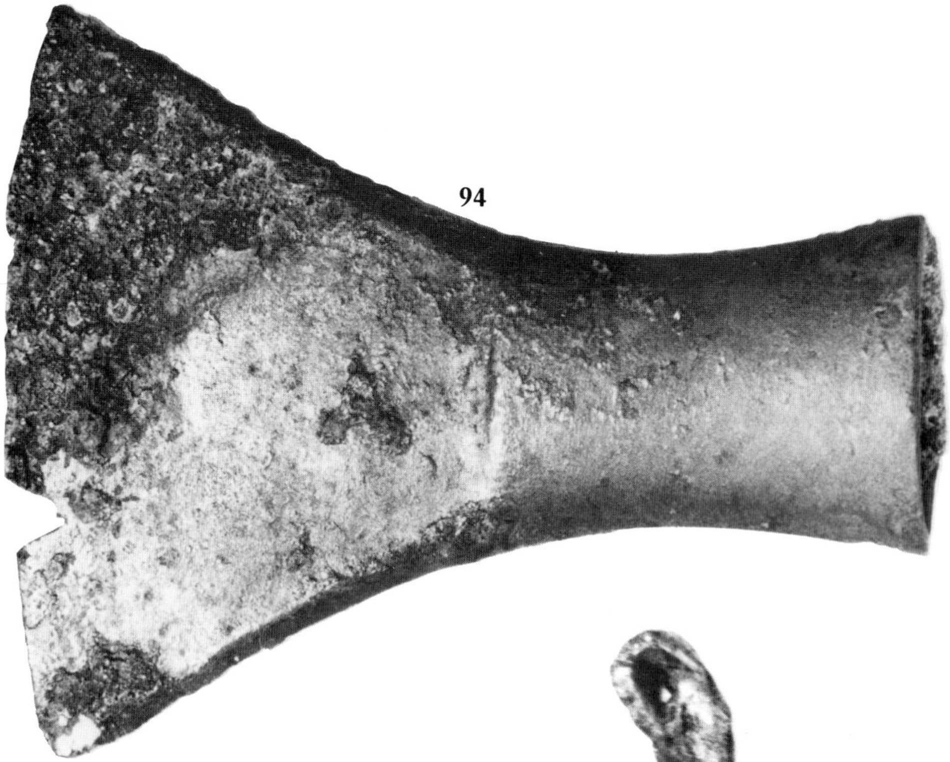

94

99

97

98

96

102

104

96. **Point** ca. 1700–1400 B.C.
bronze
l: 2.4 cm; w: 1.2 cm
BT SF 799/S1565

97. **Hook** ca. 1700–1400 B.C.
bronze
l: 4.0 cm
BT SF 890/S1696

Excavations at a site called Ban Tong located about seven kilometers south of Ban Chiang produced these two small bronze items, a hook (possibly a fishing hook) and a point. Deriving from levels with dates equivalent to the Early Period at Ban Chiang (ca. 1700–1400 B.C.), these objects show that the early metalsmiths of the Ban Chiang tradition made bronze into small utilitarian items as well as the larger more elaborate bangles and bivalve axes and spearpoints.

98. **Bracelet** Middle Period
ca. 800–400 B.C.
bronze
d: 4.7 cm
Burial 16, BCES SF 491/1286

99. **Anklet** Middle Period
ca. 800–400 B.C.
bronze
d: 6.3 cm
Burial 16, BCES SF 492/1286

100. **Bracelet** Middle Period
ca. 800–400 B.C.
bronze
d: 4.8 cm
Burial 14, BCES SF 1239/1114

101 **Bracelet** Middle Period
ca. 800–400 B.C.
bronze
d: 4.0 cm
Burial 23, BCES SF 495/1438

102 **Bangle** Late Period (?)
bronze
d: 5.0 cm
BC SF 704/1557

Bronze bangles worn either as anklets or as bracelets are highly characteristic of the Ban Chiang metallurgical tradition. They were found on children at least as often as on adults, perhaps more often. While the bronze bangles from the Early Period are simple rings (cat. nos. 93, 95), those of the Middle and Late periods show greater elaboration in cross section, shape, and surface design. No molds for these bangles were recovered during excavation. Analysis of samples cut from the bangles shows they were cast, but received no postcasting treatment such as hammering or annealling. It is likely they were made by the lost wax process.

103. **Bracelet** Middle Period
ca. 1000–400 B.C.
bronze
d: 9.9 cm
Burial 40, BCES SF 591/1981

This style of bracelet, a stunning example of a flanged bangle with a T-shape cross section, is found widely throughout East Asia in various media aside from bronze, such as stone (fig. 49, cat. no. 163). In fact the middle-aged man wearing this bangle had a matching one made of calcite (cat. no. 140). His other grave goods included white carinated and painted and incised pottery (cat. nos. 39–41), and one animal figurine (cat. no. 49).

104. **Three Bangles** Middle Period (?) ca. 800–400 B.C.
bronze
d: 6.8 cm. (ave.)
BC SF 708/1594

These three remarkable bangles, which were separated only after conservation was completed, were clearly made to be worn as a set (fig. 48). The external surfaces of the outer rings are contoured in the shape of scallops, while the internal ring is merely notched along the outer edge to match these scallops. Similar concern for matching sets of items is evident in the grave furnishings of Middle Period burials.

106

105

105. **Spearpoint (Fragment)**
Middle Period
ca. 800–400 B.C.
iron blade with bronze socket
l: 10.9 cm; w: 3.4 cm
BCES SF 548/1582

106. **Spearpoint** Middle Period
ca. 800–400 B.C.
iron blade with bronze socket
l: 28.7 cm; w: 3.6 cm
Burial 24, BCES SF 573/1813

These bimetallic (two metal) spearpoints (cat. nos. 105, 106, fig. 46) contain some of the earliest smelted, wrought iron known from East Asia. X-rays and metallographic analyses of samples cut from the blade and hafts have shown how these objects were made. Low nickel content indicates that the iron was smelted from ores. The blade was then hammered (wrought) into shape. The bronze socket was subsequently cast onto an iron nub extending from the blade. A few bimetallic artifacts are also encountered during the earliest transitional stages to the Iron Age in both China and the Near East. The ancient metalsmith might have combined the bronze, originally yellow, with the iron, originally black, for aesthetic reasons since, according to the metallurgists, bimetallic spearheads were not necessarily technologically superior products. These spearpoints were associated with Middle Period burials overlain by sherd sheets.

107. **Bracelets** Middle Period
ca. 800–400 B.C.
bronze with iron
d: 5.4 cm
Burial 26, BCES SF 532/1601

108. **Bracelet** Middle Period
ca. 800–400 B.C.
iron
d: 5.4 cm
Burial 26, BCES SF 531/1601

109. **Bracelets (Fragment)** Middle Period ca. 800–400 B.C.
iron
d: 5.9 cm
d: 5.4 cm
Burial 26, BCES SF 530/1601

110. **Bracelets** Middle Period
ca. 800–400 B.C.
iron
d: 5.3 cm; l: 5.2 cm
Burial 26, BCES SF 533/1601

Art can serve as an experimental medium for new technologies, hence it is noteworthy that among the earliest iron objects from Ban Chiang are ornamental bangles. These bracelets (cat. nos. 107–110) adorned the arms of a five-year-old child who lay in a sherd sheet of shattered carinated pots. This individual also wore a bronze bangle with decorative bosses and scoring over which iron rings were either wrapped or slipped and corroded into place (cat. no. 107). Since iron has not survived as well as bronze, the original shapes and surfaces of iron objects are less well known.

111. **Bell** age unknown
bronze
l: 3.1 cm; d: 2.8 cm
BC SF 716/2016

This large spiral-decorated bell was found on the surface of the first season's excavation at Ban Chiang. Other bells (cat. nos. 112–114) have been found in isolated contexts in levels of the Late Period; none have yet been found with a burial. Thus we have little direct evidence for the ancient use of these bells. However, large bells have been found attached to bracelets from unprovenienced contexts (see cat. no. 168).

107

112. **Bell** Late Period
ca. 300 B.C.–A.D. 200
bronze
l: 1.6 cm; d: 1.3 cm
BCES SF 162/203

113. **Bell** Late Period
ca. 300 B.C.–A.D. 200
bronze
l: 1.8 cm; d: 1.1 cm
BCES SF 254

114. **Bell** Late Period
ca. 300 B.C.–A.D. 200
bronze
l: 1.7 cm; d: 1.2 cm
BCES SF 725/2511

Two of these bronze bells have loops for attachment to strings. The means of attachment for the third is broken off. The clapper, a bronze ball, still remains inside catalogue number 112. Bells similar to these continue to be made by the lost wax process by groups in the Philippines (Newman 1977). Wax wire is twisted into the spiral shapes which are attached to sprues, channels through which the wax will flow out. The bells are then embedded in the mold paste made of pounded rice, charcoal, and clay. When the mold is fired, the wax runs out the sprues and the mold is ready for the molten bronze to be poured into a spout. After the bronze solidifies, the mold is broken away, liberating the bells. These can then be strung onto necklaces.

115. **Wire (Fragment)**
ca. A.D. 1-100
bronze
l: 7.1 cm
Burial 3, DK SF 214/S388

The quantity of jewelry adorning one five-year-old child at Ban Chiang led to her being given the very modern nickname "Bianca." Although excavators found her multistrand necklace of thin twisted and straight filaments to be virtually dust, small fragments were retrieved. Their analysis revealed a sophisticated type of bronze with a high proportion of tin—more than 20 percent. Specialized manufacturing techniques were undertaken to make such thin strands of this bronze, which if treated as the low tin bronzes would be extremely brittle. This particular fragment of high, or *beta,* tin bronze came from the site of Don Klang near Non Nok Tha from levels dating to about A.D. 1 to 100.

The presence of these sophisticated bronze wires in the Late Period of Ban Chiang and related sites shows the continued precocity and distinctiveness of the Southeast Asian metallurgical tradition.

Worked Bone Artifacts of Ban Chiang

116. **Carved Antler** Early Period
ca. 1500–100 B.C.
bone
l: 4.2 cm; w: 3.1 cm
BCES SF 527/1593

117. **Bangle (Fragment)** Early Period ca. 2000–1500 B.C.
bone
l: 5.1 cm; w: 3.0 cm
BCES SF 632/2139

118. **Bangle (Fragment)** Early Period ca. 2000–1500 B.C.
bone
l: 2.3 cm; w: 2.4 cm
Burial 56, BCES SF 675/2295

119. **Bangle (Fragment)** Early Period ca. 2000–1500 B.C.
bone
l: 3.1 cm; w: 2.4 cm
Burial 56, BCES SF 720/2295

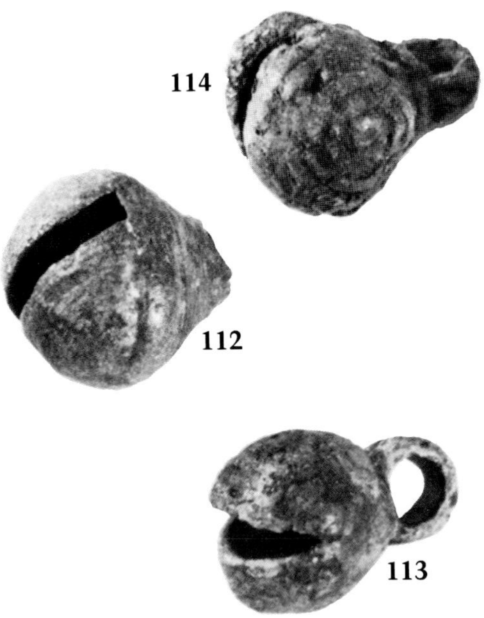

114

112

113

111

116

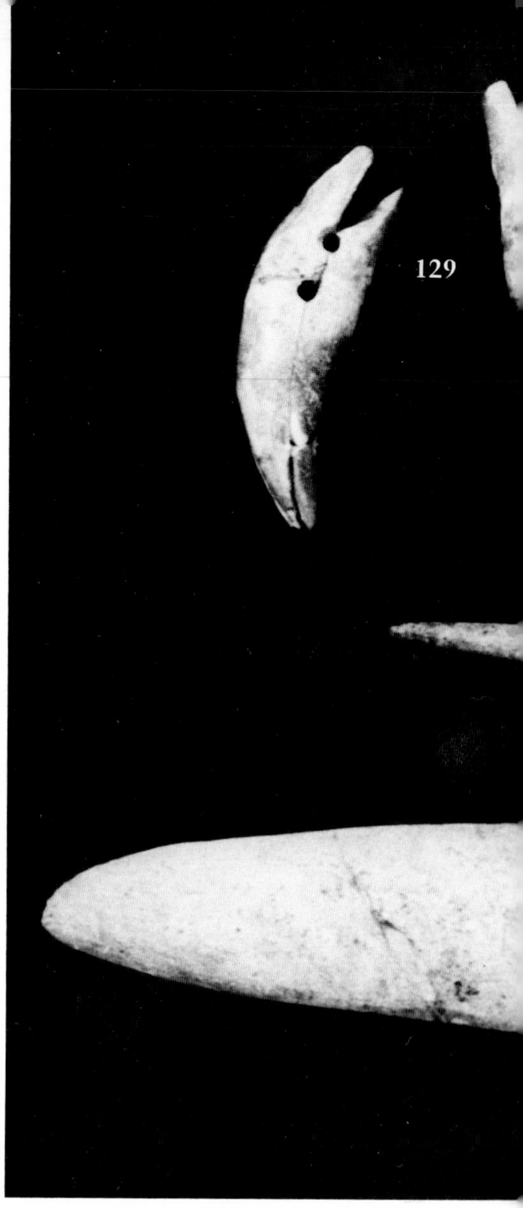

129

120. **Bangle (Fragment)** Early Period ca. 2000–1500 B.C.
bone
l: 2.2 cm; w: 2.2 cm
BCES SF 1348/1617

121. **Bangle (Fragment)** Middle Period ca. 1000–300 B.C.
bone
l: 5.5 cm; w: 2.7 cm
BCES SF 396/1125

122. **Worked Antler** Middle Period ca. 1000 B.C.
bone
l: 13.6 cm; w: 2.4 cm
BCES SF 476/1355

123. **Bangle (Fragment)** Middle Period ca. 1000 B.C.
bone
l: 1.5 cm; w: 2.2 cm
BCES SF 620/1998

121

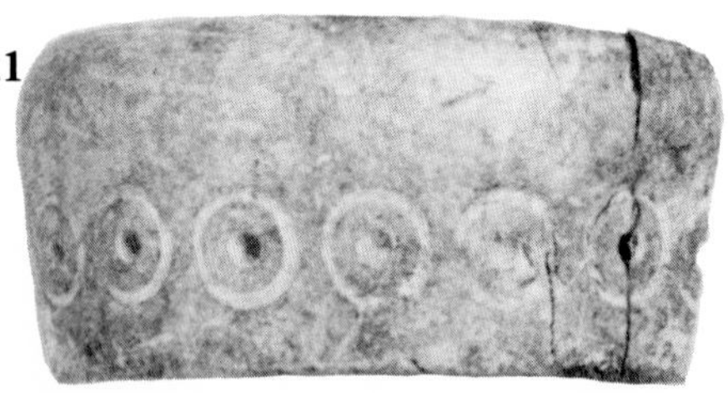

117

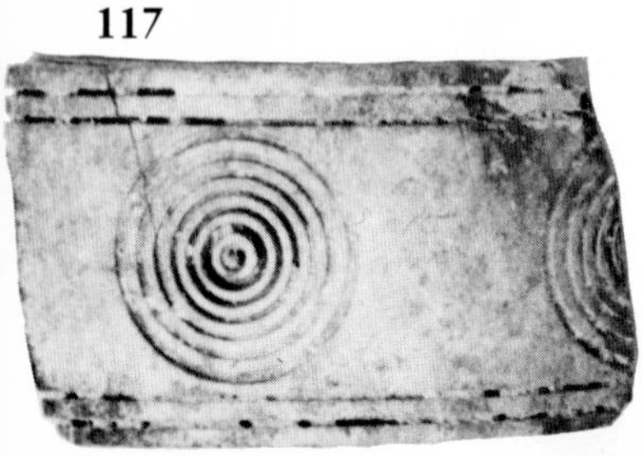

123

120

119

118

124. **Ring** Late Period ca. 300 B.C.–A.D. 200
Antler
l: 3.0 cm; d: 3.4 cm
BCES SF 331/890

125. **Pointed Tool** 1700–1400 B.C.
bone
l: 12.1 cm; w: 0.7 cm
BT SF 817/S1447

Pieces of bone which have in some way been fashioned were commonly found during the excavation, but their ancient role is often enigmatic. With the striking exception of "Nimrod's" grave goods (cat. nos. 126–129), these bone artifacts are usually found outside of burials in the general deposit and hence lack contextual clues to their meaning. While intuitively one suspects that the semicircular fragments with carved concentric circles (cat. nos. 117–121, 123) were most likely bracelets, the purpose of such items as bone "pins" (cat. no. 125) or rings (cat. nos. 116, 124), some quite exactingly carved, remains open to speculation.

126. **Hair Pin** Early Period ca. 1500 B.C.
bone
l: 17.8 cm; w: 0.7 cm
Burial 20, BC SF 2018/905

127. **Spearpoint** Early Period ca. 1500 B.C.
bone
l: 28.2 cm; w: 4.1 cm
Burial 20, BC SF 2026/1032

128. **Carved and Drilled Antler** Early Period ca. 1500 B.C.
bone
l: 11.5 cm; w: 3.8 cm
Burial 20, BC SF 2025/1032

129. **Two Pendants** Early Period ca. 1500 B.C.
tiger teeth
l: 8.1 cm; w: 2.2 cm
l: 6.9 cm; w: 2.0 cm
Burial 20, BC SF 2024/1032

This unique set of artifacts (cat. nos. 126–129, fig. 52), all of bone, was placed with a tall, muscular young man dubbed "Nimrod" after the biblical hunter. A carved tanged bone spearpoint (cat. no. 127) was found by his left wrist, the carved and drilled antler (cat. no. 128) of mysterious purpose, by his left elbow. Over his neck, as though they had been draped as pendants, were two drilled tiger's teeth (cat. no. 129), and along the right side of his skull a carved and drilled bone pin (cat. no. 126) suggested a means to tie up long hair. While the precise social meaning for his grave furnishings is elusive, their singularity suggests that this individual was recognized by the ancient society not so much for his wealth as for his role, deeds, or perhaps even his character.

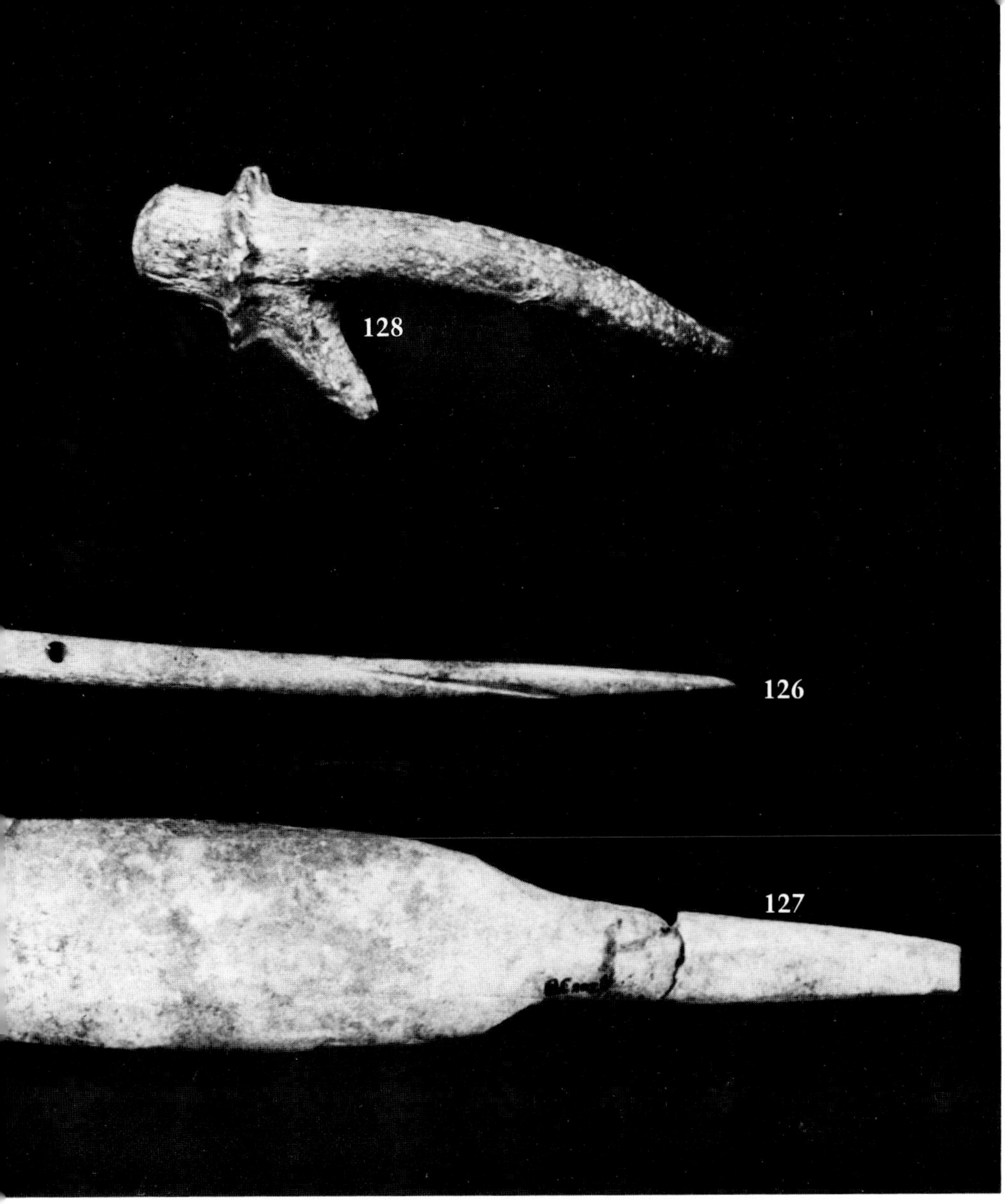

Stone Artifacts of Ban Chiang and Related Sites

130. **Adze/Axe** Early Period
ca. 1500–1000 B.C.
stone
l: 2.2 cm; w: 1.4 cm
BCES SF 514/1520

131. **Adze/Axe** Middle Period
ca. 1000–300 B.C.
stone
l: 7.8 cm; w: 4.3 cm
BCES SF 338/911

132. **Adze/Axe** Late Period
ca. 300 B.C.–A.D. 200
stone
l: 2.8 cm; w: 1.5 cm
BC SF 800/13

133. **Adze/Axe** Late Period
ca. 300 B.C.–A.D. 200
stone
l: 5.1 cm; w: 3.8 cm
BC SF 821/1215

134. **Adze/Axe** Late Period
ca. 300 B.C.–A.D. 200
stone
l: 3.5 cm; w: 3.5 cm
BC SF 836/1586

135. **Adze/Axe** Late Period
ca. 300 B.C.–A.D. 200
stone
l: 4.7 cm; w: 2.2 cm
BCES SF 130/143

136. **Adze/Axe** ca. 2000 B.C.
stone
l: 4.2 cm; w: 2.9 cm
BPT SF 86/S179

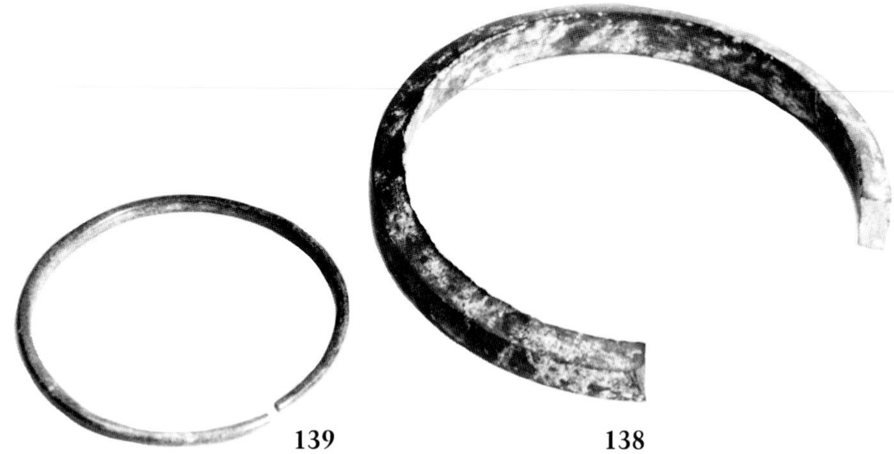

139

138

137. Adze/Axe
ca. 1000 B.C.–A.D. 1
stone
l: 6.8 cm; w: 5.5 cm
BT SF 467/S758

Prior to extensive scientific excavation in Southeast Asia, attempts to define the prehistory of the region depended heavily on the distribution of adze types found in surface collections. Thus it is ironic that not only have few adzes been recovered from Ban Chiang and related sites, but also that these adzes are usually small and irregularly shaped. Their rarity may be due to sample bias, i.e., when adzes were abandoned, worn out, or lost, they were generally deposited outside funerary and habitation areas subsequently excavated. On the other hand, stone adzes may have had a minor role in a culture that had access to bronze adzes.

These examples (cat. nos. 130–137) show the range in size and shape of adzes excavated at Ban Chiang and nearby sites. Probably used for woodworking, most are simple four-sided shapes with the exception of one shouldered adze (cat. no. 134). Local sources for the fine-grained stone are not known. Thus they most likely were imported, possibly as part of a trade network that also distributed copper and tin. The delineation of this ancient trade network is one of the most important research topics for future prehistoric research in northeast Thailand.

138. Bangle (Fragment)
age unknown
stone
d: 6.3 cm
BPT SF 98/S

139. Bangle A.D. 1–100
stone
d: 3.8 cm
DK SF 124/S320

In addition to adzes, bangles were also commonly made from fine-grained green stone and seem to be found from the Early to the Late Periods. Unlike bronze bangles, however, they were not recovered from burial contexts and hence are usually in a fragmentary condition. Most have a quadrangular cross section, although one beautiful thin "C" ring (perhaps an earring) was recovered from a Ban Chiang related site of Don Klang (cat. no. 139).

140. Bangle (Fragment) Middle Period ca. 1000–400 B.C.
calcite
l: 3.5 cm; w: 2.1 cm
Burial 40, BCES SF 592/1981

This fragment of a flanged, "T" section bangle was worn next to a bronze bracelet of the same style (cat. no. 103). The bangle was made from calcite as was determined by Dr. Ohashi at the Department of Geology, University of Pennsylvania. Since calcite is not locally available, it must have been imported. The style of bangle is found widely throughout Southeast Asia (see cat. no. 163).

Unprovenienced Artifacts Possibly of the Ban Chiang Tradition

Most of the following catalogue entries come from contexts outside of scientific excavations. Some came from surface collections. Some were donated to the National Museum of Thailand by Thai citizens. Some were confiscated by the police in accordance with the 1972 Thai law prohibiting sale of Ban Chiang antiquities. These objects are included in the exhibition to illustrate the richness and diversity of the Ban Chiang cultural tradition, and also to illustrate how much knowledge is lost when these items are haphazardly removed from their stratigraphic contexts. While one may appreciate their variety and fanciful designs, the articles themselves are mute on their ages, sources, their makers and users. Given the lively industry in faking and repairing, even their authenticity is in some cases questionable. Although some comparisons with the excavated artifacts can be made, more impressive is the distinctiveness, great variety, and superb condition of these objects. Since the professional excavation produced proportionally few intact artifacts, the amount of fragmentary, perhaps more humble, but still enormously informative, artifactual material which must have been destroyed in order to retrieve even one stunning pot is staggering and appalling. So many questions remain about this extraordinary ancient culture. Will the evidence stay in place long enough for the archaeologist to retrieve and decipher it?

141. Pot
ceramic
h: 17.1 cm; d: 25.2 cm
National Museum of Thailand 474/2521

Curvilinear incised pot with punctate impressions, appliqué, and ring foot.

141

142

142. Pot

ceramic

h: 37.7 cm; d: 44.2 cm

National Museum of Thailand 373/2520

No black curvilinear incised pots of this shape were excavated at Ban Chiang. The flare of the upper body and the flange are, however, reminiscent of the beaker type pots.

143. Pot

ceramic

h: 23.6 cm; d: 29.2 cm

National Museum of Thailand 251/2519

Ring based pots with appliqué have not been found with curvilinear painted designs in the archaeological record.

144

145

148

151

144. **Pot**
ceramic
h: 21.2 cm; d: 29.4 cm
National Museum of Thailand 246/2519

White carinated pots comparable to this one have been found archaeologically only in a shattered state.

145. **Pot**
ceramic
h: 22.8 cm; d: 19.4 cm
National Museum of Thailand 215/2515/117

No painted and incised pedestaled pots like this were excavated by the NETAP project at Ban Chiang.

146. **Pot**
ceramic
h: 26.0 cm; d: 19.7 cm
National Museum of Thailand 382/2520

A web motif is painted around the white scrolls of this red-on-buff round bottomed pot.

147. **Pot**
ceramic
h: 22.8 cm; d: 24.2 cm
National Museum of Thailand 46/2518/3

The curling forms which decorate the body of this pot have been interpreted as stylized water buffalo.

148. **Pot**
ceramic
h: 27.7 cm; d: 23.6 cm
National Museum of Thailand 250/2519

Painted medallions and other geometric designs adorn this round bottom pot with flaring rim.

149. **Pot**
ceramic
h: 24.5 cm; d: 24.2 cm
National Museum of Thailand 83/2516

Restored red-on-white painted pot with concentric design (fig. 9).

150. **Pot**
ceramic
h: 25.6 cm; d: 22.7 cm
National Museum of Thailand 247/2519

Near the juncture of the lower body and base of this pot are stylized representations of deer (?) (fig. 33, 34). These are rare examples of depictions of natural forms.

151. **Pot**
ceramic
h: 51.0 cm; d: 42.0 cm
National Museum of Thailand 418/2521

Round bottomed red-on-buff painted pot.

152. Pot
ceramic
h: 41.7 cm; d: 47.8 cm
National Museum of Thailand PB 1

Just under the rim of this huge, round-bottomed pot were painted horizontal stylized representations of human figures, a rare example of the depiction of the human form.

152 (detail)

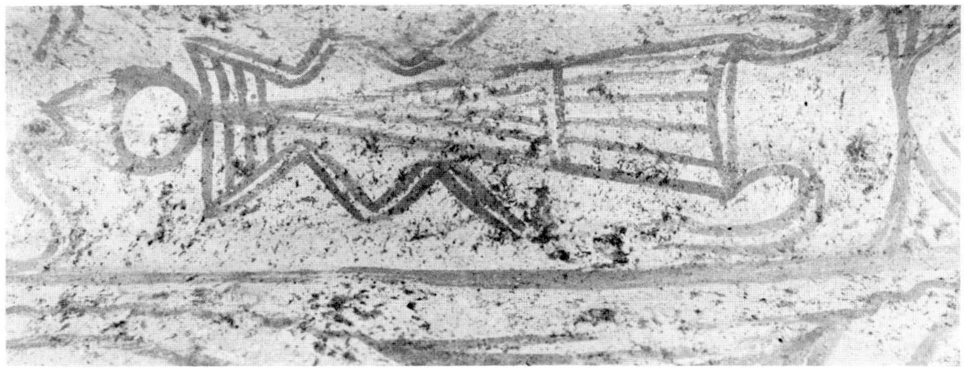

152

153

155

156

158

157

153. Pot
ceramic
h: 34.0 cm; d: 31.5 cm
National Museum of Thailand 390/2520

The shape of this pot is supposedly characteristic of pots from sites in Sawang Daeng Din, an area adjacent to the Ban Chiang county, but no pots of this shape have been found at Ban Chiang.

154. Pot
ceramic
h: 45.1 cm; d: 35.8 cm
National Museum of Thailand 35/2521

Painted red-on-buff round bottomed pot.

155. Roller
ceramic
l: 8.5 cm; d: 3.0 cm
National Museum of Thailand 236/2515/7

156. Roller
ceramic
l: 3.5 cm; d: 2.8 cm
National Museum of Thailand 225/2515/42.2

157. Roller
ceramic
l: 4.3 cm; d: 3.1 cm
National Museum of Thailand 36/2518/4

158. Roller
ceramic
l: 5.5 cm; d: 2.5 cm
National Museum of Thailand 8/2517/78

These rollers show variation in designs, but since they lack context they do not help resolve their role in ancient life. Catalogue number 155 has a pattern similar to a Ban Chiang excavated roller (cat. no. 71).

154

159

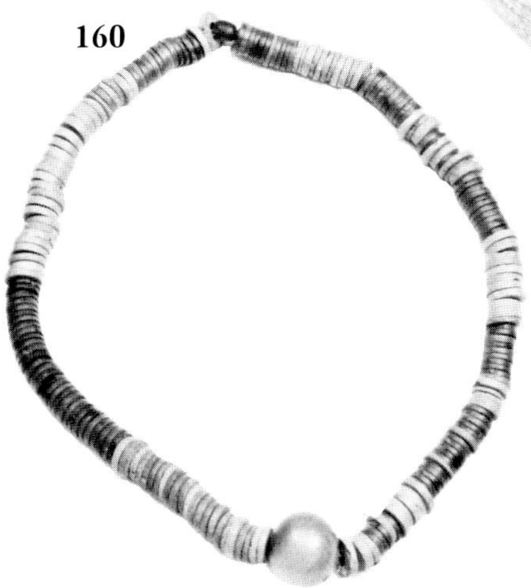

160

161

159. Ladle
ceramic
l: 23.2 cm; w: 12.6 cm
National Museum of Thailand 246/2515

160. Bead Necklace
glass
d: 14.8 cm
National Museum of Thailand 225/2515/4

161. Bead Necklace
glass
d: 11.1 cm
National Museum of Thailand 225/2515/3

163

166. Bangles with Cloth
bronze and fiber
l: 7.1 cm; d: 4.0 cm
Anonymous lender

Forearm bones ringed with bronze bangles were characteristic of early items coming out of the Ban Chiang sites and sold on the antiquities market. The set of eleven plain bronze bangles encircling a child's forearm (fig. 10, cat. no. 165) was purchased by a Westerner from a Ban Chiang villager before the 1972 Thai law against the selling of Ban Chiang antiquities went into effect. The human bones at first frightened the villagers who feared malevolent ghosts until it was explained that the bones came from pre-Buddhist times. These bangles, given to The University Museum, helped to stimulate interest in investigating the unknown bronze age. The bangles with adhering cloth (cat. no. 166) were donated to the project by an anonymous Thai. Such preservation of organic fibers is very rare.

162. Bead Necklace
glass
d: 12.2 cm
National Museum of Thailand 132/2516

Glass beads are popular on the antiquities market. Few were recovered during NETAP excavations.

163. Bangle
stone
d: 10.0 cm
National Museum of Thailand 129/2516

This beautiful flanged marble bracelet is comparable in style to a bronze one (cat. no. 103) excavated at Ban Chiang (fig. 49).

164. Bivalve Axe Mold with Two Modern Casts
sandstone and plaster
h: 15.0 cm; w: 12.0 cm (mold)
h: 14.7 cm; w: 7.8 cm (two casts)
National Musuem of Thailand 136/2516 and 137/2516

This mold shows an asymmetrical style of axe with no excavated parallel.

165. Bangle with Forearm Bones
bronze and bone
l: 17.5 cm; d: 8.0 cm
Lent by The University Museum 72-20-1

167. Three Bangles
bronze
d: 6.7 cm (ave.)

Found on a low burial of a pilot excavation in Ban Chiang. These and other bronze bangles suggested that a fullscale excavation at Ban Chiang would help understand the early Bronze Age in northeast Thailand.

168. Bangle with Bells
bronze
d: 9.2 cm
National Museum of Thailand 130/2516

168

166

171

169. Bangle with Bells
bronze
d: 7.1 cm
National Museum of Thailand 225/2515/22.2

These two bracelets with paired sets of bells suggest how the isolated bells excavated at Ban Chiang dating to the Late Period (cat. nos. 111–114) may have been used. Spiral pattern bells similar to these are still made by groups in the Philippines (Newman 1977). It is not known when such bells ceased to be made in Thailand.

170. Bangle
bronze
d: 8.0 cm
National Museum of Thailand 225/2515/23

Bronze bangle with knobs around the edge and traces of cloth is reportedly from Ban Chiang.

171. Bangle
bronze
d: 8.0 cm
National Museum of Thailand 219/2515/42

Bangle with bosses around both edges and braided cord surface design.

172. Neckband
bronze
d: 13.7 cm
National Museum of Thailand 192/2516

Large round neckband with opening reportedly found at Ban Phon Sung.

173. Spearpoint
bronze
l: 37.0 cm; w: 6.0 cm
National Museum of Thailand 549/2517

The age and source for this magnificent socketed spearpoint are unknown. It was reconstructed from four pieces donated to the National Museum of Thailand.

173

Ethnographic Objects

175

174

174. Ladle
bronze
l: 32.6 cm; w: 8.9 cm
National Museum of Thailand 2200/2518

Many unique artifacts like this long handled bronze ladle which derive from unprovenienced contexts have no parallel from archaeological excavations. Thus the age and context for this item can not even be guessed. Impressions of rice husks on the corroded surface have little scientific value without knowing the date and source for the ladle itself.

175. Bracelets with Arm Bones
ivory and bone
h: 7.2 cm; l: 15.2 cm
BPT SF 2049

These bangles were given by villagers to archaeologists on survey.

176. Pellet Bow
bamboo, jute, and rattan
l: 110.5 cm; w: 3.3 cm
Lent by The University Museum 82-7-1

Small spherical baked clay balls called pellets (cat. no. 36) commonly found at Ban Chiang tradition sites might have been ammunition for a weapon similar to this pellet bow. This one was made by an elderly man in a village near Ban Chiang. The bow went out of use about fifty years ago in the Ban Chiang region. The string of this bow is split and a tiny platform is woven of rattan at the midpoint against which a small round object can be grasped for shooting. Since a pellet bow is made entirely from organic materials it would not survive in most archaeological contexts.

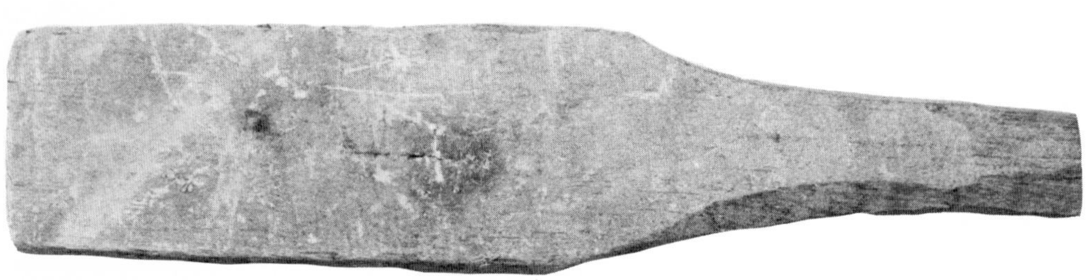

177

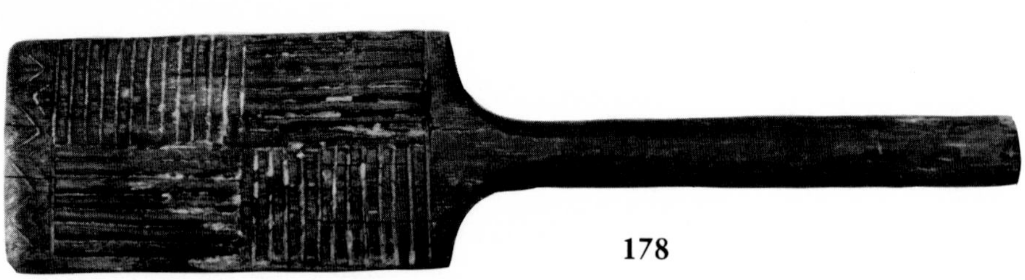

178

177. Paddle
wood
l: 28.7 cm; w: 6.3 cm
Lent by The University Museum 82-7-3

178. Paddle
wood
l: 24.8; w: 5.6 cm
Lent by The University Museum 82-7-2

179. Anvil
ceramic
l: 9.3 cm; w: 8.3 cm
Lent by The University Museum 82-7-5

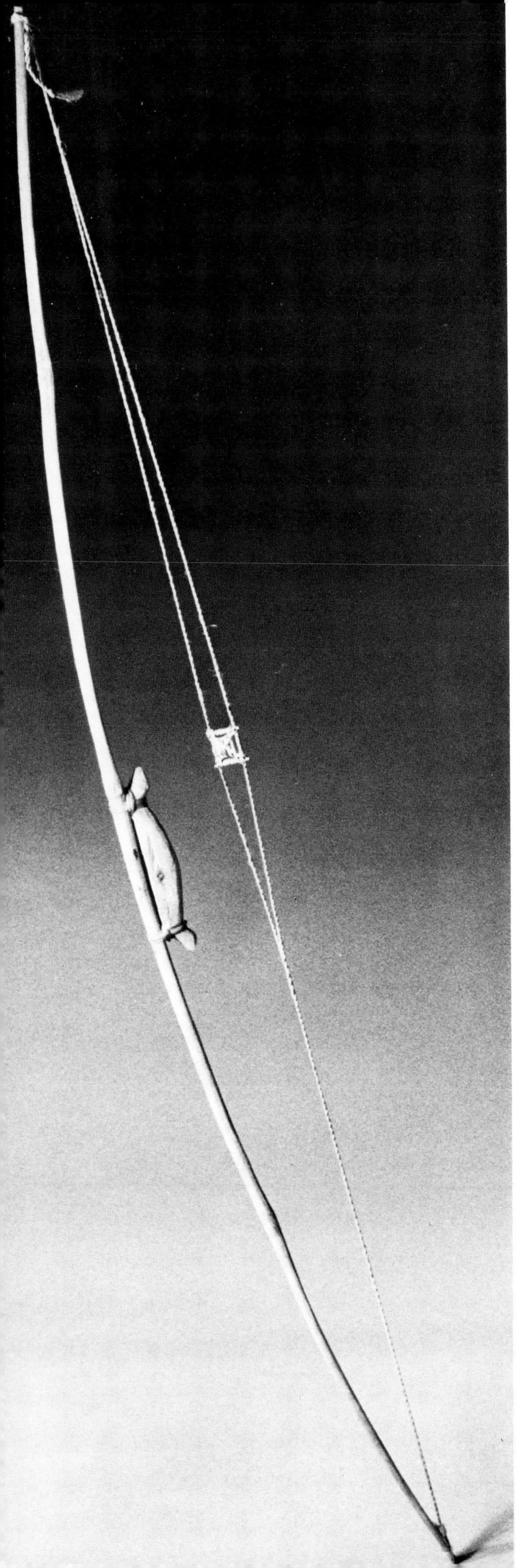

176

180. **Anvil**
ceramic
l: 4.4 cm; w: 5.3 cm
Lent by The University Museum 82-7-4

181. **Anvil**
ceramic
l: 15.2 cm; w: 11.5 cm
Lent by The University Museum 82-7-6

The study of traditional pottery manufacture in the Ban Chiang region today helps in understanding the ancient ceramic technology. These pottery anvils (cat. nos. 179–181) collected from modern-day potters are very similar to items excavated from Ban Chiang and related sites (cat. nos. 86–89). Presumably, wooden paddles comparable to those of today (cat. nos. 177, 178) would have been used by the ancient potter as well.

REFERENCES

Bayard, Donn T.

1971 *Non Nok Tha: The 1968 Excavation Procedure, Stratigraphy, and a Summary of the Evidence.* University of Otago: Studies in Prehistoric Anthropology, vol. 4.

1972 Early Thai bronze: Analysis and new dates. *Science* 176: 1411–12.

1977 Phu Wiang pottery and the prehistory of northeastern Thailand. In *Modern Quaternary Research in Southeast Asia,* G. Bartstra, W. A. Casparie, and I. C. Glover, eds., pp. 57–102. Rotterdam: A. A. Balkema.

1979 The chronology of prehistoric metallurgy in North-east Thailand: *Silābhūmi* or *Samrddhabhūmi?* In *Early South East Asia Essays in Archaeology, History, and Historical Geography,* R. B. Smith and W. Watson, eds., pp. 15–32. New York: Oxford University Press.

1980 *The Pa Mong Archaeological Survey Programme, 1973–75.* University of Otago: Studies in Prehistoric Anthropology, vol. 13.

Bellwood, Peter

1979 *Man's Conquest of the Pacific.* New York: Oxford University Press.

Benedict, Paul K.

1975 *Austro-Thai Language and Culture with a Glossary of Roots.* New Haven: HRAF Press.

Blust, Robert

1976 Austronesian culture history: Some linguistic inferences and their relations to the archaeological record. *World Archaeology* 8: 19–43.

Charoenwongsa, Pisit

1978 Early Southeast Asian bronze in the light of excavation in Thailand. In *Bronze Culture in Asia,* pp. 53–76. Tehran: Asian Cultural Documentation Centre for UNESCO.

1982 Ban Chiang in retrospect: What the expedition means to archaeologists and the Thai public. *Expedition* 24(4): 13–15.

Chi-lu, Chen

1968 *Material Culture of the Formosan Aborigines.* Taipei: The Taiwan Museum.

Clark, Grahame

1971 *World Prehistory: A New Outline.* Cambridge: Cambridge University Press.

Clark, J. G. D., and S. Piggott

1965 *Prehistoric Societies.* London: Hutchinson.

Coedes, G.

1966 *The Making of Southeast Asia.* Berkeley: University of California Press.

Colani, Madeleine

1927 L'age de la pièrre dans la province de Hoa-Binh (Tonkin). *Memoires de la Service Geologique d'Indochine* 14.

Darlington, C. D.

1963 *Chromosome Botany and the Origin of Cultivated Plants.* London.

Davidson, Jeremy H. C. S.

1975 Recent archaeological activity in Viet-nam. *Journal of the Hong Kong Society* 6: 80–99.

1979 Archaeology in northern Vietnam since 1954. In *Early South East Asia Essays in Archaeology, History and Historical Geography,* R. B. Smith and W. Watson, eds., pp. 98–124. New York: Oxford University Press.

de Candolle, Alphonse

1883 *Origine des Plantes Cultivées.* Paris.

Evers, Hans-Dieter, ed.

1969 *Loosely Structured Social Systems: Thailand in Comparative Perspective.* Cultural Report Series no. 17. New Haven: Yale University.

Glover, Ian C.

1977 The Hoabinhian: Hunter-gatherers or early agriculturalists in South-East Asia? In *Hunters, Gatherers and First Farmers Beyond Europe,* J. V. S. Megaw, ed., pp. 145–66. Leicester University Press.

1980 Ban Don Ta Phet and its relevance to problems in the pre- and protohistory of Thailand. *Bulletin of the Indo-Pacific Prehistory Association* 2: 16–30.

Gorman, Chester F.

1969 Hoabinhian: A pebble-tool complex with early plant associations in Southeast Asia. *Science* 163: 671–73.

1970 Excavations at Spirit Cave, North Thailand: Some interim interpretations. *Asian Perspectives* 13: 79–107.

1981 A case history: Ban Chiang. *Art Research News* 1(2): 10–13.

Gorman, Chester F., and Pisit Charoenwongsa

1976 Ban Chiang: A mosaic of impressions from the first two years. *Expedition* 18(4): 14–26.

Hastings, John

1982 Potsherds into printouts: The Ban Chiang computer project. *Expedition* 24(4): 37–41.

Hayden, Brian

1977 Sticks and stones and ground edge axes: The upper palaeolithic in Southeast Asia? In *Sunda and Sahul: Prehistoric Studies in Southeast Asia, Melanesia and Australia,* J. Allen, J. Golson, and R. Jones, eds., pp. 73–109. New York: Academic Press.

Heine Geldern, R. von

1951 Das Tocharerproblem und die Pontische Wanderung. *Saeculum* 2: 225–55.

1954 Die Asiatische Herkunft der Sudamerikanischen Metalltechnik. *Paideuma* 5: 347–423.

Higham, Charles, and Amphan Kijngam

1979 Ban Chiang and northeast Thailand: The palaeoenvironment and economy. *Journal of Archaeological Science* 6: 211–33.

1982 Prehistoric man and his environment: Evidence from the Ban Chiang faunal remains. *Expedition* 24(4): 17–24.

Higham, C. F. W., A. Kijngam and B. F. J. Manly

1980 An analysis of prehistoric canid remains from Thailand. *Journal of Archaeological Science* 7: 149–65.

Higham, C. F. W., A. Kijngam, B. F. J. Manly, and S. J. E. Moore

1981 The bovid third phalanx and prehistoric ploughing. *Journal of Archaeological Science* 8: 353–65.

Hoffman, Carl

1982 Implications of economics: The "wild Punan" of Borneo. Preliminary research report presented to Lembaga Ilmu Pengetahuan Indonesia (unpublished).

Kijngam, Amphan, Charles Higham, and Warrachai Wiriyaromp

1980 *Prehistoric Settlement Patterns in North East Thailand.* University of Otago: Studies in Prehistoric Anthropology, vol. 15.

Li, Hui-lin

1970 The origin of cultivated plants in Southeast Asia. *Economic Botany* 24: 3–19.

Lyons, Elizabeth, and Froelich Rainey

1982 The road to Ban Chiang: A dialogue of events leading to The University Museum's participation in the expedition. *Expedition* 24(4): 5–12.

Maddin, Robert, J. D. Muhly, and T. S. Wheeler

1977 How the Iron Age began. *Scientific American* 237(4): 122–31.

Moore, Frank J.

1974 *Thailand: its People, its Society, its Culture.* New Haven: HRAF Press.

Newman, Thelma R.

1977 *Contemporary Southeast Asian Arts and Crafts.* New York: Crown Publishers, Inc.

Pearson, Richard

1962 Dong-So'n and its origins. *Bulletin of the Institute of Ethnology Academia Sinica* 13: 27–52.

Penny, James S., Jr.

1982 Petchabun piedmont survey: An initial archaeological investigation of the western margins of the Khorat Plateau. *Expedition* 24(4): 65–72.

Pietrusewsky, Michael

1978 A study of early metal age crania from Ban Chiang, Northeast Thailand. *Journal of Human Evolution* 7: 383–92.

1981 Cranial variation in early metal age Thailand and Southeast Asia studied by multivariate procedures. *Homo* 32: 1–26.

1982 The ancient inhabitants of Ban Chiang: The evidence from the human skeletal and dental remains. *Expedition* 24(4): 42–50.

Pittioni, Richard

1970 Spectro-analytical research in bronze from northeastern Thailand. *Asian Perspectives* 13: 158–61.

Sauer, Carl O.

1952 *Agricultural Origins and Dispersals.* New York: American Geographical Society.

Saurin, E., and J. P. Carbonnel

1974 Evolution prehistorique de la peninsule Indochinoise d'après les Données Recentes. *Paleorient* 2: 133–65.

Schauffler, William

1976 Archaeological survey and excavation of Ban Chiang culture sites in Northeast Thailand. *Expedition* 18(4): 27–37.

1979 Computerized data base management systems in archaeological research: A SELGEM case study. *MASCA Journal* 1(2): 50–55.

Selimkhanov, I. R.

1979 The chemical characteristics of some metal finds from Non Nok Tha. In *Early South East Asia: Essays in Archaeology, History and Historical Geography,* R. B. Smith and W. Watson, eds., pp. 33–38. New York: Oxford University Press.

Smith, Cyril Stanley

1973 Bronze technology in the East: A metallurgical study of early Thai bronzes, with some speculations on the cultural transmission of technology. In *Changing Perspectives in the History of Science: Essays in Honor of Joseph Needham,* M. Teich and R. Young, eds., pp. 21–32. London: Heinemann.

Solheim, Wilhelm G., II

1968 Early bronze in northeastern Thailand. *Current Anthropology* 9: 59–62.

1971 New light on a forgotten past. *National Geographic* 139: 330–39.

Stech Wheeler, Tamara, and Robert Maddin

1976 The techniques of the early Thai metalsmith. *Expedition* 18(4): 38–47.

van Esterik, Penny

1981 *Cognition and Design Production in Ban Chiang Painted Pottery.* Ohio University Center for International Studies, Southeast Asia Series no. 58.

van Esterik, Penelope, and Nancy Kress

1978 An interpretation of Ban Chiang rollers: Experiment and speculation. *Asian Perspectives* 21: 52–57.

van Heekeren, H. R.

1958 *The Bronze-Iron Age of Indonesia.* 's-Gravenhage: Martinus Nijhoff.

Vavilov, N. I.

1926 Studies in the origin of cultivated plants. *Bulletin of Applied Botany* 16: 139–248.

White, Joyce C.

1982 Natural history investigations at Ban Chiang: The study of natural resources and their use today aids reconstruction of early village farming in prehistory. *Expedition* 24(4): 25–32.

i.p. Ethnoecological research aids the reconstruction of prehistoric environment and subsistence in Northeast Thailand. *South-East Asian Studies Newsletter.*

White, Joyce C., Lois Kratz, Cheryl Applebaum, and Deborah Wong

1982 Processing the Ban Chiang finds: With particular reference to volunteer and student work at The University Museum. *Expedition* 24(4): 33–36.

White, Joyce C., and Chester F. Gorman

1979 Patterns in "amorphous" industries: The Hoabinhian viewed through a lithic reduction sequence. Paper presented at the 44th annual meeting of the Society for American Archaeology, Vancouver, British Columbia.

Workman, D. R.

1972 *Mineral Resources of the Lower Mekong Basin and Adjacent Areas of Khmer Republic, Laos, Thailand and Republic of Vietnam.* United Nations: Mineral Resources Development Series no. 39.

Yen, Douglas E.

1977 Hoabinhian horticulture: The evidence and the questions from northwest Thailand. In *Sunda and Sahul: Prehistoric Studies in Southeast Asia, Melanesia and Australia.* J. Allen, J. Golson, and R. Jones eds., pp. 567–99. New York: Academic Press.

1982 Ban Chiang pottery and rice: A discussion of the inclusions in the pottery matrix. *Expedition* 24(4): 51–64.

Catalogue production coordinated by Andrea Stevens

Book design by Dennis R. Pollard, Washington, D.C.

Studio photographs by Joan Broderick

Field photographs courtesy of The University Museum

Composed in Trump by Carver Photocomposition, Inc.
Arlington, Virginia

Printed on Warren's Lustro Offset Enamel dull
by Eastern Press, New Haven, Connecticut